MORE *than* ENOUGH

Aunt Trulaa,

There are not words adequately to express the wonderful ways you've enriched my life. Thank you!

Love
Da

MORE *than* ENOUGH

DON FORRESTER

TATE PUBLISHING
AND ENTERPRISES, LLC

Published by Tate Publishing & Enterprises, LLC
127 E. Trade Center Terrace | Mustang, Oklahoma 73064 USA
1.888.361.9473 | www.tatepublishing.com

Tate Publishing is committed to excellence in the publishing industry. The company reflects the philosophy established by the founders, based on Psalm 68:11,
"The Lord gave the word and great was the company of those who published it."

Book design copyright © 2015 by Tate Publishing, LLC. All rights reserved.
Cover design by Charito Sim
Interior design by Jimmy Sevilleno

Published in the United States of America

ISBN: 978-1-68118-429-6
1. Family & Relationships / General
2. Biography & Autobiography / Personal Memoirs
14.12.20

THIS BOOK IS dedicated to Treva Topper Forrester whose life, love, companionship, and support has always been More Than Enough.

CONTENTS

PREFACE

Too often life is lost in living. When life is grasped and valued for the experience, the associated memories highlight lessons learned and the joys associated with taking none of it for granted.

I chose the title "More than Enough" for my life adventure. Despite the routine and commonplace of the treasured gift I call my life, I have discovered that God's providential grace and support have always been more than enough to see me through. It was the apostle Paul who wrote, "But he said to me, 'My grace is sufficient for you, for my power is made perfect in weakness.' Therefore I will boast all the more gladly about my weaknesses, so that Christ's power may rest on me" (2 Corinthians 12:9).

PLAY IT FORWARD

THE NEWSPAPER REPORTER telephoned to set the appointment. When she arrived, she said she had come to interview me about my life, my interests, and my family. She was not seeking information about the agency where I worked. That was my first surprise. I was prepared to talk about my work.

Her next question also surprised me: "Is there any lesson you learned in childhood that you still remember?" I didn't have to give it a moment's thought before I enthusiastically responded, "Absolutely! Don't play with dynamite!" This time, I could see from her face that she was the one who was surprised.

I went on to explain that as a sixth-grader, I was one of three boys conducting a science experiment in front of the class. We unknowingly detonated a blasting cap of dynamite. I'll never forget the long red and yellow wires that came out of the end of what looked like a tube of lipstick. One of us had found it walking from home to school that day. We were smart kids. We thought it was an electromagnet. All we needed was a dry-cell battery to make it work. We had one, and it did. It certainly proved to be an explosive way to end a school day. The mistake was costly.

We each spent at least a week in the hospital and another two weeks recuperating at home. Lesson learned: "Smart kids don't play with dynamite."

With her nod of approval, indicating that I was giving her the kind of information she was looking for, I found myself completely relaxed. I welcomed her next question and was totally at ease with the interview. She subsequently was very kind in her written assessment. I smiled when I saw that she had described me as "a child at heart." She went on to say, "Fueled by energy like that of a three-year-old after a hunk of birthday cake, this perky, good-humored sixty-two-year-old zings between his many roles...." It was a very complimentary article.

She also shared what I told her regarding my approach to life. I credited Leo Buscaglia for establishing the mind-set, but it has worked well for me all of my adult life. "If you act crazy consistently, you can get by with anything. Otherwise, they call the cops." I remember reading that and finding that it resonated with my spirit. Perhaps rather than giving me a new approach, it described and validated what intuitively has always worked well for me.

Fifty years after the explosion at school, I assisted my parents in packing their household when they moved from the hometown where I grew up. In the midst of senior adulthood, they needed the support associated with having family near. Consequently, at my insistence, they chose to move a couple of miles from where I live. I was delighted. While packing up their home to get it ready for the movers, I found a shoebox filled with get-well cards and notes from my sixth grade classmates. Truthfully, I didn't remember receiving the cards and well wishes.

Reading through them drew me back to a world that seemed long ago and far away. I smiled when I read some of the handwritten notes. The general theme related to well wishes for a speedy recovery and the notion that I was missed at school. Some classmates commented that I was really funny and they missed having me in class. It wasn't nearly as much fun without me.

For as long as I can remember, humor and laughter have defined my life. I sometimes jokingly say that the approach is one of my spiritual gifts. Perhaps? Perhaps not? At any rate, it is a great tool to negotiate all the demands associated with living.

I recently told someone that nonsense comes easy for me; it's the complicated stuff that slows me down. I've never tried my hand at stand-up comedy, but I seldom overlook an opening to interject something that solicits laughter. Generally people like to laugh. I've used humor as long as I can remember to negotiate conflict, resolve problems, manage difficulty, entertain friends, and relate to others.

While I was in college, I worked part-time as a technician in the emergency room of a large hospital. It was a real learning experience for me. I witnessed individuals and families of all ages in the midst of great difficulty and trauma. Four decades later, I can still vividly remember witnessing much that was unsettling and sad. But one of the things I most remember from the experience is the camaraderie and support the emergency room staff provided one another. It was an incredible antidote against second-hand trauma. It was not uncommon for doctors, nurses, and other emergency room staff to congregate in one of the interior offices of the emergency room suite when things were not busy. Without fail, we'd find something to laugh about. Laughter proved to be an incredible tool to rejuvenate our emotions and reduce our stress levels.

I didn't think about it at the time, but years later, I've reflected back on the experience with disturbing surprise at what was commonplace during that time. For one thing, ambulance service was limited to a "tote and transport" kind of experience. Ambulances were little more than station wagons and were not equipped with medical personnel or equipment. In addition, at least in the city where I worked, the ambulance service was provided by the funeral homes in that town. I can't think of a more poignant example of a conflict of interest.

A couple of years after graduating from college, I found myself as a twenty-three-year-old child welfare worker doing child abuse investigations and working with children and families in crisis. I loved the work, but once again, I found myself in an environment where a major survival method to deflect the second-hand trauma was one of laughter. We endearingly referred to it as child-welfare hysteria.

Across a lifetime, I've made another observation regarding the advantage of following Leo Buscaglia's recommended formula for embracing life with humor. "If you act crazy consistently, you can get by with anything. Otherwise they call the cops." When you take that approach, people don't expect much. When you get it right, they are amazed.

It is important that I confess to you up-front that I don't always get it right. Sometimes I do. Sometimes I don't.

A couple of years ago, I participated in an iSpeak training course related to public speaking. As an introduction and warm-up for the class, we were asked to quickly write a six-word memoir. The assignment was to identify six words that best represent our life. It proved to be a tougher assignment than I initially imagined, particularly with the clock ticking and not having much time to reflect. My first thought quickly gravitated to something my wife has said. She routinely tells me "tongue in cheek" that if I precede her in death, she will ensure that my tombstone is marked "He always did it his way." Perhaps without knowing, she has already written the most appropriate six-word memoir to describe me.

When the assignment was made, I wasn't familiar with the concept of six-word memoirs. Reportedly, the concept originated under the inspiration of Ernest Hemmingway's legendary shortest of short stories, "For Sale: Baby Shoes, Never Worn."

What six words would I choose? It took a few moments, but I came up with the following:

- *"Relational."* I place a high emphasis on the ability to connect with people and the privilege of being connected with God. I am most at peace when I sense connection in both venues.

- *"Adventuresome."* I don't want to miss any of life. I want to live life with a sense of adventure and expectation.

- *"Funny."* I value laughter. When it comes to nonsense, I'm at the top of my game.

- *"Kind."* Someone told me a long time ago to always be gentle with others. Everywhere you look, folks are having a difficult time. There is not a better witness to the indwelling spirit of Christ than kindness. We talk about God's grace, but talk is cheap. We need to demonstrate God's grace and that comes through kindness.

- *"Broken."* I don't always get it right. Despite my best intentions, I am sometimes disappointing. (When someone asks me what I do at work, I generally respond that I do the best that I can.)

- *"Redeemed."* If it weren't for God's grace, I'd be a total wreck. Fortunately, I am the recipient of his grace.

Despite the fact that there are a number of strengths that define my life, that is only a part of the story. I don't always get it right. The apostle Paul wrote, "I do not understand what I do. For what I want to do I do not do, but what I hate I do" (Romans 7:15). What is true for Paul is also true for me.

As I shared in the preface, I chose the title "More than Enough" for my life adventure. Despite the repetitive shortcomings, failures, inadequacies, and disappointments in my life, I have found that God's providential grace and support have always been more than enough to see me through. It is abundantly true that His power is made perfect in weakness.

Following my son's graduation from college and commissioning in the United States Marine Corps, he wrote me an incredibly kind letter complimenting me for being his dad and thanking me for the way I've lived my life. Craig stated that he had obviously over-identified with what he learned of my twin brother during his growing up years. My brother's plane went down in Vietnam during the Christmas bombing raids of 1972, and he was subsequently listed as MIA. Craig was only a year old at the time.

Craig grew up with an extended family that did everything they could to keep my brother's memory in the forefront. I, too, was an advocate to make that happen. Forty years later, I am still dedicated to supporting my brother's legacy with a sense of gratitude for the time we shared.

When it was time to select a college to attend, it was an easy choice for my son. He went to Texas A&M, found his place in the Corps of Cadets, and received his commission in the US Marine Corps, just like my brother. He even wore my brother's senior boots.

The letter stated that despite my brother's wonderful accomplishments, I was the real hero in his life. I was greatly humbled and deeply touched by the undeserved compliment.

I responded to his letter with a profound level of gratitude and thanksgiving. I went on to write that what I find most troublesome is that "if he knew me better, he wouldn't like me as well." I was quick to note that I have no interest in confessing my shortcomings and cautioned him not to even ask. I guess it is simply a tangible example of the biblical promise, "My power is made perfect in weakness." I don't always get it right.

I don't always get it right. The reality of that simplistic truth was recently reinforced for me. I was scheduled to provide training for our staff. The training topic related to the importance of trauma-informed care when working with children who come from hard places. We now know through research that ongoing abuse and neglect in early childhood years negatively impacts brain development and ultimately impairs every facet of a child's life. It is only through relationship building, establishing trust, ongoing connection, and repetitive patterning of appropriate behavior that the child can move beyond the limitations of his or her past. There are no shortcuts to wholeness.

Because of the importance of the topic, coupled with my desire to come across as someone who has a good working knowledge of the subject, I spent all day two days before the training fine-tuning my notes and developing a PowerPoint presentation. By the end of the day, I felt pretty good about what I had crafted.

I was covered up with a series of meetings the following day. As it turned out, the morning was nonstop, and the afternoon was dedicated to more meetings focused on the next year's budget. Somehow toward the end of the day, I found a thirty-minute interval to log on to my computer. For my own peace of mind, I wanted to quickly go over the information I had prepared for the training for the following morning.

Did I mention I don't always get it right? What I discovered is that none of the work I had done two days before was saved on our network drive. As I headed to the last meeting of the day, I was experiencing a sense of panic. Is it possible that I failed to save any of the documents on my computer? What about the PowerPoint? It was really a good presentation. Was it also gone? Panic became second nature to me.

As it turned out, because of another commitment, I didn't get home until around 9:30 or 10:00 p.m. that evening. I quickly checked my computer at home. I looked at my desktop and also logged in again to the office network. Nothing was there.

Calf rope! I give up! I was beat! I told my wife I was going to go to bed. I would get to the office early the next morning, review some notes I had made earlier, and hope for the best.

I did manage to get up early. I got ready for work, packed for an out-of-town trip, and was headed out the door before 6:00 a.m. I anticipated being at work by 7:00 a.m. The training didn't start until nine thirty. That would give me two-and-one half hours. It wasn't optimal, but it was all right. I would have it all together by nine thirty.

Did I mention I don't always get it right? I had traveled at least twenty miles from home when I discovered I didn't have my cell phone. A sense of panic reemerged.

- Do I turn around and go back home? Do I really have to have my phone?
- Can I live without the phone calls and e-mail?
- Initially, I thought yes and drove through the first good place to turn around. Panic immediately set in. I had to have my phone. I was leaving town later in the day.
- I turned around at the next good place and made my way back home.

It was probably eight fifteen to eight thirty before I actually made it to work. About fifteen minutes later, there was an announcement on the intercom that the first chapel service of the new school year began at 9:00 a.m. Bummer! I had the thought, "I don't have time for this," but I went anyway. I'm not really sure I had a choice.

The person who introduced the chapel program for the group leading the chapel service indicated the topic for the morning was prayer. She then said we were going to experience several things:

- First, we were going to practice silence.
- We were going to focus on several different scriptures.
- We were going to listen to meditative music.
- We were going to focus on thoughts related to prayer.

Social workers. Sometimes as a group, they are a little too nontraditional for me. I had an immediate flashback to the last time this group led chapel. They passed out Crayolas and paper and had us spend our time drawing something related to our thoughts concerning God. Oh brother! Was this going to be a waste of time?

As it turned out, it was the perfect venue for calming my fears, preparing my thoughts, and trusting that God was going to ensure that the training fell into place. After all, the whole concept of connection, relationships, and wholeness comes from God. There is nothing I can add to improve on that.

The focus of the chapel experience related to God's intent that we be *connected* to him. We make that connection through the leadership of the Holy Spirit. Two of the ways it manifests itself is through prayer and meditation.

By the time chapel was over, you would have thought I'd been injected with a sedative. I have never been more at peace. There was absolutely no anxiety related to the training. The experience of worship served as an incredible backdrop to talk about the importance of connection.

God wants us to be connected to him. He wants us to be connected to others. The only hope to promote healing for children from hard places is to equip them with the ability to be connected.

On some mornings, I listen to a radio talk show on my way to work. Recently I heard a "Waiting by the Phone" episode, where a caller is distraught because some anticipated response, action, or expression of kindness has not taken place. The radio station initiates an on-the-air call to the individual who has not met the caller's expectations and inquires why. The individual who is the participant in "Waiting by the Phone" is also on the line to hear the response. Honestly, you'd have to be certifiably crazy or have "Stupid" tattooed on your forehead to be desperate enough to have a radio station attempt to intercede in your behalf.

The caller the morning I was listening was distraught because a very close friend was getting married and she had not been asked to serve as a bridesmaid. I listened long enough for the person called to answer the phone and then be told the nature of the call before I turned the radio off. I didn't want to hear what I envisioned would be a very awkward and painful telephone conversation for one of the two parties.

Unfortunately, I didn't wait long enough before I turned the radio back on. I heard the sound of, "I'll wear my hair like a poodle if that's what you want. I just want to honor you by being your bridesmaid." Apparently the reason the person was not asked to be in the wedding party was because the bride-to-be wanted a certain look in her wedding pictures. The caller was more of a tomboy and her look would be incongruent with the preferred style of the day.

The conversation left a sick sensation in the pit of my stomach. How superficial and shallow! I painted them both with the same broad brush. Sadly, the reality is that many folks relationally don't have any more regard for others than that.

Later in reflecting on the "Waiting by the Phone" episode, the thought occurred to me, "I wonder if God is ever puzzled when I'm unavailable or not attentive to his desire for communication with me. How many times in the course of a day or week do I fail to have a sense of his indwelling spirit and for all practical purposes am unreachable?"

I have been fortunate in my life to be surrounded by capable, compassionate, caring, and exceptionally skilled individuals. It is true in my work environment, home environment, church environment, and neighborhood. If I were to be perfectly honest with you, I'd acknowledge that I like my life. However, I'm still very much a work in progress. I don't always get it right.

A friend recently asked me about my interest in baseball. After all, it has been said that baseball is the all-American sport. He seemed a little surprised when I told him I have been boycotting baseball since I was nine years old. My twin brother and I both tried out for the First State Bank Little League team in the town where we lived. He made the team. I did not.

Despite the fact that my brother and I were close, we were also destined to be competitive. Strangers would see the two of us together and ask questions like, "Who's the smartest?" "Who's the fastest?" "Who's the toughest?" It was almost as though we struggled to define our own identity by excelling against the other in one area or another. I laughingly told someone the other day that I probably needed therapy to resolve the feelings of inadequacy I experienced when I didn't make the Little League baseball team at the age of nine while my brother was selected for the team.

Actually, the coaches made a good call. I was a lousy baseball player. My brother, on the other hand, was very good. During the tryouts, I would stand in left field praying to God that no one would hit a ball in my direction. At the same time, my brother was playing first base and praying that the ball would be hit in his direction.

Despite the fact that I really didn't want to play baseball, it was the expectation in my peer group that I should. After all, it is the all-American sport. Being excluded from the team was painful on one level and a relief on another.

Thirty years later, I ran for school board in the small community where my son attended school. We were relatively new to the community, but serving on the school board was something I really desired to do. The school system was antiquated, and I could envision any number of positive changes that could be made to enhance the programs and opportunities for students. When the votes were counted, the vote did not go my way. I was disappointed. I had a flashback to being nine years old and excluded from what was considered the norm of my day. Everybody played baseball.

Too often, self-esteem is wrapped up in accomplishment and being at the top of the leaderboard in one's profession or social standing. Unfortunately, there are many more of us that meet the criteria for being considered "common" than those who clearly excel. Only a few demonstrate levels of giftedness that propel one into the limelight of greatness.

I recently read *My Lord, What a Morning*, the autobiography of Marian Anderson. She was an incredibly gifted and musically talented individual who grew up with a background of poverty and racial discrimination. Despite the obstacles that came her way, she excelled in her giftedness and her ability to maintain a level of highest respect.

- One review of her book stated, "An entire chapter devoted to the Easter concert at the Lincoln Memorial in 1939 reveals Anderson's immense respect for Eleanor Roosevelt, who resigned from the Daughters of the American Revolution when they refused to let Anderson perform at Constitution Hall. Supplanting sorrow and regret for anger and violence, Anderson demurely imparts her views on discrimination and on becoming an icon in the struggle for civil rights."

- In 1955, she became the first African American to sing with the Metropolitan Opera Company in New York City.

- The next year, her autobiography was written: *My Lord, What a Morning*. It became a best seller.

- In 1958, she became a US delegate to United Nations.

- On several occasions, she was given the highest medals awarded by foreign countries.

- She was called to the White House to sing to the Roosevelts and the crowned heads of England.

- In Philadelphia, she received a ten-thousand-dollar Bach award as the citizen who brought the most distinction to that city.

- In 1963, she was given the coveted Presidential Medal of Freedom.

A newspaper reporter once asked Marian Anderson, "What is the highest moment, the greatest achievement of your life?" Her response didn't include any of the aforementioned honors. She stated simply, "The greatest moment of my life was when I went home and told my mother she wouldn't have to take in washing anymore."

I like the way the Kirkus Review of *My Lord, What a Morning* expressed it, "There is a quiet beauty in this retiring, almost dutiful reminiscence of a life. Marian Anderson tells her story with the simplicity and dignity and graciousness people have come to associate with her."

The question asked of Marian Anderson is one that continues to linger in my head long after reading the book. "What is the highest moment, the greatest achievement of your life?" How would you respond if that question were asked of you? I've given much thought to it, and the only honest answer I can make is, "It hasn't happened yet." My life is mostly routine and commonplace. That is not synonymous with uneventful and boring. I like my life. It is full and eventful, but there is nothing about my life that could be described as exceptional. I put my trousers on one leg at a time. My work has variety, but it is not rocket science.

Someone told me years ago that perhaps the most significant contribution that we can make is simply to show up. That being said, I am content to play it forward and trust that God will be glorified in the process. I am holding on to the promise that his power is made perfect in weakness. It really is more than enough.

IT IS ALL ABOUT
THE ADVENTURE

IT WAS FIVE years ago. I remember it like it was yesterday. Ours was a small group, and I am sure that I looked out of place. There were eight of us. I was the only person in the group with gray hair. I was easily twenty years older than the next oldest member. The majority appeared to be in their early twenties. The thing we shared in common was our inability to ski. Obviously we had a vested interest in learning how to get down the mountain without killing ourselves. I had never skied before, but I was confident I could learn. In my younger years, I had thoroughly enjoyed waterskiing. Could the skill set really be that different?

Shortly after the ski lesson began, the group was standing in a straight line listening to the instructor commenting on our successful completion of our third training step. I'm not sure what I was doing as he spoke. As I recall, I was only trying to scoot over a couple of feet, but embarrassingly, I found myself toppled over lying in the snow. Without missing a beat, the instructor announced that step four was learning how to get up once we had fallen down. He then instructed me to get up. That proved more difficult than I imagined. He said it would work best if I took one ski off first and did it that way. Wow! It did prove to be much easier.

By the time we were ready to ride the ski lift and began making our way down the mountain, I was feeling a little more confident. However, I had already determined that the skill set for snow skiing was completely different from waterskiing. This was uncharted territory for me.

Once we were off the lift, the instruction was for us to ski to an identified point and then wait for the remainder of the group. It didn't take long for me to conclude that a couple of folks in our group would have had difficultly walking down the mountain without skis. It was clear that this group lesson was going to be a "hurry up and wait" kind of experience while those most challenged by gravity were attempting to rejoin the group.

Despite periods of waiting, it was an incredibly exhilarating experience. Much to my surprise, the ability to make turns and zigzag my way to the next identified point was filled with excitement and wonder over the amount of fun inherent in the experience. When we were finally given permission to ski back to the beginning point and get in line for the ski lift again, I easily made my way far in front of others in the group.

This time, the ski instructor and I rode back up the mountain in the same chair lift. He asked me if I'd skied before and said I was "smoking" the rest of the group. That was really a boost to my self-confidence. It was like giving me carte-blanche approval to be a little more daring and ski a little closer to the edges of the path before making my turns. He called it skiing in parallel lines. I was not familiar with the concept, but it seemed like the only comfortable way to get the most out of the experience. After all, who wants to ski in a wedge position all the way down the mountain?

The four hours of instruction flew by, and I was ecstatic with the prospect of being on the threshold of a new adventure.

I awakened early the next morning. As I drank my first cup of coffee and waited for daylight, I reflected back over the experience of the previous day and thought about the exhilaration and satisfaction found in snow skiing.

It occurred to me that I want that same sense of adventure in every facet of my life. I don't want to just get by and settle for business as usual. I want to soak it up and squeeze every ounce of joy that can be gained. I want to live life in relationship with others and with God in such a way that nothing is left that can be gained. I want it all. I want to live life passionately and with a sense of excitement that I'm wasting none of it.

Business as usual for so many people is a level of boredom that is closely akin to an inability to walk down the mountain much less negotiate it on skis with a sense of excitement, joy, and fulfillment.

Dr. Bernie Siegel has a chapter in one of his books entitled, "Living in the Moment." I like the way he expresses it, "Live your life now. Don't waste it. Everybody dies, but there are too many people who never live."

He went on to say, "When I work with people, I ask them questions that I think help clarify for me what kind of people they are and get them to look at their lives quickly. The first question I ask is, 'Do you want to live to be 100?' The people who respond with a yes are saying, 'I'm not afraid of the future. I'm not afraid of outliving everyone I love. I'll find new people to love. I'm not afraid of illness and aging. I'm looking at the world with a different viewpoint.' And they are the kind of people who survive."

I would like to think that I am open to living to be one hundred. However, I recently had a strange experience that I found a little unsettling. I had a doctor's appointment. I was seeing a new doctor, so I had downloaded all the needed forms required for completion and brought them with me for my appointment.

The nurse walked into the examining room and said, "Let me get the computer. I've got some questions we need to go over." He left to get the computer and came back into the room and logged in.

Once the computer was up, he turned to me and said, "So you're eighty-five?" It took me a moment to realize he was asking me a question.

I responded, "I beg your pardon."

He replied, "So you are eighty-five. You were born in 1927."

My first thought was "What kind of a nut are you? You've got to be kidding! Are you taking mind-altering medications or do you need glasses?" I was also hopeful the new doctor had better assessment skills and better bedside manners.

Instead of verbalizing my thoughts, I decided to just go with it. I responded, "That's right. I'm eighty-five years old, and I really think I'm doing well for a man my age. I am still pretty agile. I can get in and out of my car without difficulty. I still drive. I have a high energy level, and I guess, overall, I try to take good care of myself. What other questions do you have?"

He looked at me like he thought I was on mind-altering medications, so I confessed that I was joking. (I didn't express my first thought which still was unchanged—"he was nuts") I told him I wasn't born in 1927. I was born in 1947. By the way, he didn't seem to have much of a sense of humor. I don't think he was amused or that he even thought my response was funny.

Shortly before his death at the age of ninety-six, my grandfather said to me, "Don, it goes by quickly." I am increasingly discovering the truthfulness of his assessment. Time does seem to fly by quickly.

It seems like the New Year just started. In the blink of an eye, it is already mid-February. I don't know about you, but I didn't give myself permission to make any new New Year's resolutions this year. However, I did give myself permission to start living differently. The two resolutions left over from the previous year continue to be a part of my dream:

- I want to create wonderful memories with my grandchildren and

- I want to reconnect with some people who have been significant in my life that I've not had an opportunity to visit with in a very long time.

I want my grandchildren and the significant others in my life to know they are important to me and that the ongoing gift of their friendship and love has greatly enhanced my life. After all, the people in our lives are the only things we have that are eternal.

Those two leftover resolutions plus giving myself permission to live differently if I need to will provide the catalyst in establishing priorities related to how I spend my gift of time.

At the risk of revealing one of my character flaws, I have to confess that Christmastime is not my favorite time of the year. I love the message of Christmas, the birth of Christ, the gift of God, the availability of life everlasting. I cherish that message, and I love the reason for the season, but Christmas is not my favorite time of the year. Every year as the holiday season approaches, I have the passing thought that I wish I could hit the fast forward button and hold it down until sometime in January.

This past December was different. It emerged into an exceptional experience of unprecedented Christmas joy in our home. Very early on a Monday morning, I opened Facebook. A simple one-line status caught my attention. It was written by my son, "After six and a half months, I am finally out of Afghanistan." (Note: It had only been a year between deployments. The year before, he returned from Afghanistan following a thirteen-month deployment. He received the Bronze Star in recognition of his military service related to that assignment. From a parent's perspective, enough is enough!)

Wow! I sat teary-eyed at my computer for a few minutes. I looked at the clock. It was 5:00 a.m. My wife isn't known for heavy drama, but when I told her about the status, she immediately started crying. I couldn't help but wonder, "What is wrong with us? This is the best news ever, and it came a couple of weeks earlier than we were anticipating."

I didn't spend a lot of time wondering where my son was when he made his Facebook status. It really didn't matter. Wherever he was had to be safer than where he had been. Later that night, I was reviewing comments to his Facebook status and found that he subsequently responded to a comment, stating, "I am in Germany watching it snow..." That put a smile on my face. At one time, my son and his family were stationed in Northern California where snow defined the winter lifestyle. That is where I took my first ski lesson.

Three days later, my son was safely home in North Carolina. His wife decided his early arrival back home would be a great surprise for their children, but she wanted to make the surprise even more special. She picked my grandchildren up from school, and when they returned home, there was a very large box wrapped in Christmas paper, sitting in their driveway. My daughter-in-law's proclamation that someone had brought them a present was all they needed to hurry from the car to the box.

When asked if they wanted to open it, the oldest and youngest said, "Yes!" The middle child suggested they wait until Christmas. The "yes" votes won, and they immediately started tearing off paper. There were three very surprised and very happy children when they discovered their dad.

I talked with my youngest grandson the next day. He excitedly said, "Granddad, my dad is home today! He popped out of a box!" Once again, I was teary-eyed.

My two New Year's resolutions left over from the previous year coupled with giving myself permission to live differently was all I needed to anticipate a wonderful new year.

My wife and I welcomed the New Year by meeting our son and his family at a ski resort in Virginia.

The snow skiing wasn't quite what I anticipated, but I'd do it again in a heartbeat. It was more closely akin to skiing on ice with a blend of snow and artificial snow on the surface. Did I mention you can go really fast when you are skiing on ice? The good news is, I was able to get up every time I fell down. All three of my grandchildren took ski lessons for two days and found it exhilarating. Truthfully, at day's end, I was absolutely worn out, but I slept with a sense of contentment that I was fulfilling my dream.

In addition to two days of snow/ice skiing, I also chose to walk for exercise every day. I logged twenty-eight miles of walking that week. Wow! What a wonderful way to begin the New Year. I guess I emerged from a week off work thinking I'd continue the pattern of walking as exercise when I got back home. It didn't happen. I only walked thirteen miles the remaining three weeks of the month.

Surprisingly, I chose not to beat myself up because I opted to go to work rather than go for a walk, but I continue to give myself permission to live differently.

What about you? Did you make any resolutions to do things differently this year? If so, how is that working out for you?

There is an e-mail that circulated several years ago that I found delightful and thought provoking. It is entitled "Lovely Rose at 87." Perhaps you have seen it.

> The first day of school our professor introduced himself and challenged us to get to know someone we didn't already know. I stood up to look around when a gentle hand touched my shoulder. I turned around to find a wrinkled, little old lady beaming up at me with a smile that lit up her entire being. She said, "Hi handsome. My name is Rose. I'm 87 years old. Can I give you a hug?" I laughed and enthusiastically responded, "Of course you may!" And she gave me a giant squeeze.

"Why are you in college at such a young innocent age?" I asked. She jokingly replied, "I'm here to meet a rich husband, get married, and have a couple of kids."

"No seriously," I asked. I was curious what may have motivated her to be taking on this challenge at her age.

"I always dreamed of having a college education and now I'm getting one!" She told me.

After class we walked to the student union building and shared a chocolate milkshake. We became instant friends. Every day for the next three months we would leave class together and talk nonstop. I was always mesmerized listening to this "time machine" as she shared her wisdom and experience with me.

Over the course of the year, Rose became a campus icon and she easily made friends wherever she went. She loved to dress up and she reveled in the attention bestowed upon her from the other students. She was living it up.

At the end of the semester we invited Rose to speak at our football banquet. I'll never forget what she taught us. She was introduced and stepped up to the podium. As she began to deliver her prepared speech, she dropped her 3X5 cards on the floor.

Frustrated and a little embarrassed she leaned into the microphone and simply said, "I'm sorry I'm so jittery. I gave up beer for Lent and this whiskey is killing me. I'll never get my speech back in order so let me just tell you what I know."

As we laughed she cleared her throat and began. "We do not stop playing because we are old; we grow old because we stop playing.

"There are only four secrets to staying young, being happy, and achieving success. You have to laugh and find humor every day. You've got to have a dream. When you lose your dreams, you die. We have so many people walking around who are dead and don't even know it!

"There is a huge difference between growing older and growing up. If you are nineteen years old and lie in bed for one full year and don't do one productive thing, you will turn twenty years old. If I am eighty-seven years old and stay in bed for a year and never do anything I will turn eighty-eight.

"Anybody can grow older. That doesn't take any talent or ability. The idea is to grow up by always finding opportunity in change. Have no regrets. The elderly usually don't have regrets for what we did, but rather for things we did not do. The only people who fear death are those with regrets."

She concluded her speech by courageously singing "The Rose." She challenged each of us to study the lyrics and live them out in our daily lives.

At the year's end, Rose finished the college degree she had begun all those years ago. One week after graduation, Rose died peacefully in her sleep. Over two thousand college students attended her funeral in tribute to the wonderful woman who taught by example that it's never too late to be all you can possibly be.

In many respects, you and I are a work in progress. Someone wisely made the observation that "perfection is not a destination, it is a direction." We are all in the process of becoming.

I don't always get it right, but each day brings opportunities for a fresh start. The mistakes and misplaced priorities of the past don't have to dictate the future. I can opt to make better choices, use my time differently, be sensitive to God's leadership and direction, and live out the legacy that God intended.

It was the prophet Jeremiah who wrote, "'For I know the plans I have for you,' declares the Lord, 'plans to prosper you and not to harm you, plans to give you hope and a future'" (Jeremiah 29:11). The reality is each of us has work to complete. Jeremiah expressed it as "the plans I have for you." The apostle Paul clarified it when he wrote, "For we are God's handiwork, created in Christ Jesus to do good works, which God prepared in advance for us to do" (Ephesians 2:10).

Are we in touch with those plans? Do we incorporate the "good works, which God prepared in advance for us to do" into the fabric of our lives?

What is my assignment? What is your assignment? Are we engaged in God's call on our life or have we been on an extended coffee break?

Back in July, I bought a new pickup. I sold my previous truck about a year and a half ago when I feared the price of gasoline was approaching five dollars a gallon. The truth of the matter is, when you live in the country there are times you need a truck. Every time I needed a truck after I sold mine, I got a lecture from my wife on how I shouldn't have sold my truck. Consequently, I bought another one. I also thought that purchasing a truck might provide incentive for her not to lecture me anymore, but it hasn't worked.

I primarily keep the new truck in the garage. I jokingly refer to it as the vault. In order to have the truck in the garage, my work car got reassigned to the driveway. I had the passing thought recently when I opened the garage door after parking my car that I need to drive the truck more often. I've had the truck for six months. I've only driven it 338 miles. It probably needs to be driven to ensure that everything continues to work properly.

The concept of "use it or lose it" is playing heavily in my mind. I don't want to jeopardize the utility of my truck by simply keeping it in storage. Sure, it stays clean and looks new that way, but it needs to be driven.

More importantly, and this is really important, I don't want to jeopardize my ability to discern God's will and purposes for my life by being content to sit on the bench rather than becoming actively involved in the game.

The only time we have is now. The only place we have is here. Do we need to give ourselves permission to live differently?

I recently spent some time in Washington, DC. When I boarded the plane to fly home, a young man sat next to me.

Truthfully, I probably started the conversation by saying something really significant like, "It's got to be warmer in Austin than it has been here the last three days." What began as a superficial conversation turned into real communication and we talked almost nonstop for the next three hours.

He told me he was returning to Austin after spending a week visiting his family. He said he didn't get to go home for Christmas because of his work schedule. In fact, this trip was the first time he had been home since he moved to Austin six months before.

In the three hours that followed, he shared bits and pieces about his life. He moved to Austin because he thought the economy was better in Texas and that he would find more opportunities for work and advancement.

At some point in the conversation, he said, "I'm twenty-three years old, and I don't know what I'm supposed to do with my life. The only thing I know for certain is that I want to be the world's best father for my children when I have some. My parents divorced when I was young, and my dad had nothing to do with us after the divorce. Since I never had a dad, I have resolved that when I have children, I will always be there for them."

As he talked about his dad, it was almost as though he was lost in thought. He said almost to himself rather than to me, "I don't have many memories of my father." He recounted a couple or three memories and said, "That's about it. That's all I remember. I want more than that for my children."

He talked about some of the challenges associated with growing up in a single-parent household. He said, "We didn't have much money and my mother was always in school, but we had a good life. I learned the importance of family and I learned the importance of friends. That really is the only thing that matters."

In the course of our conversation, he mentioned attending church camp two or three different times. I asked him if his faith was still a support system for him. He said, "I don't really know how to answer that. It seemed more important when I was younger. I now know that making a future is up to me. I have to depend on myself. No one else can do this for me."

I replied, "You seem like a very responsible and capable young man, but you can't do it alone. Despite all of your ability, the truth of the matter is, you are not God. Only God can meet the deepest needs of your life."

- Can you imagine being twenty-three years old and not knowing why you are here?

- Can you imagine being forty years old and not knowing why you are here?

- Can you imagine being eighty years old and not knowing why you are here?

Perhaps we need to discern our real identity in Christ and seek to determine what it is that God has called us to do. If we don't do that, we will fall victim to what Mike Yaconelli describes as lethargy that results in a passionless ordinariness.

He wrote: "Our lives are filled with the clutter of activity, most of which is meaningless and unnecessary. Meetings, committees, classes, travel, television, golf, racquetball, tennis, jogging, shopping, and redecorating. We have so much to do and so little time to do it all. We soon find ourselves rushing here and rushing there while the stress of our constant rushing begins to take its toll. In order to survive the pace of our lives, we turn to superficiality and escape. We drown our stress in more activity or, eventually, in a kind of emotional lobotomy which insulates us from the passion of life. Our souls are smothered and the result is a lethargy that results in a passionless ordinariness."

The good news is that God has drafted each of us to be included in the game. It is not his intent that any of us sit on the bench. "For we are God's handiwork, created in Christ Jesus to do good works" (Ephesians 2:10). Whatever God has created for us to do, he will equip us to accomplish it if we are open to his leadership and dependent upon his support to get it done. I am holding on to the promise that "I can do all this through him who gives me strength" (Philippians 4:13). It really is more than enough.

CARPE DIEM:
SEIZE THE DAY

I DON'T THINK it is simply that I am an adrenaline junkie, but I like the sensation of speed. I probably was born with a DNA closely parallel to that of a racecar driver. I am making the assumption that the statute of limitations on speeding during adolescence and young adulthood has expired. Otherwise, I'd never admit to this in print. I received my driver's license at the age of fourteen. Subsequent to that, my parents never had a vehicle during my high school and college years that I didn't know how fast it would go.

I was always careful. I didn't drive fast on the highway unless there was virtually little traffic and I made the assessment that it could be safely done. I never weaved in and out of other vehicles. I knew that would be putting others at risk, but when the "coast was clear," the gas pedal was fully pinned to the floor of the car.

At some level, I rationalized that I was more alert and responsible at faster rates of speed. I was always careful. In addition, I never drove at excessive speeds if anyone else was in the car with me. I probably feared that somehow the information would get back to my parents. That would have been the equivalent of a death sentence.

Shortly after receiving my driver's license, I was issued a traffic ticket for not making a complete stop at a stop sign. When I returned home and told my parents that I had received a traffic ticket, my mother went ballistic. You would have thought I had been arrested for armed robbery and that I was featured on the front page of the newspaper. She immediately launched into her "this will go on your permanent record" speech and put me on notice that we were a law-abiding family and that such unlawful behavior would not be tolerated. She was really worked up. She made it clear that my behavior was unacceptable and would not be tolerated again in the future.

Fortunately for me, I had a part-time afternoon and evening job at an ice cream and hamburger shop. I was responsible for earning my own spending money. I had enough in my savings to cover the cost of the ticket. As I remember, it was a very long time before I was allowed to drive the family car unaccompanied again.

My junior year of high school, the band director at the high school invited me to go with him after school to pick up his new 1964 ½ Ford Mustang. The new Ford Mustang was featured on the cover of all the motor magazines, and I was excited to tag along. He had purchased the car from a dealership thirty miles away. The car he was trading in was a Studebaker. I don't recall the year or specific make, but it was ugly. Not only was it ugly, I also learned that it was fast. He had a tachometer mounted on the steering column. Based on his calculation, at one point, we were driving 130 miles per hour.

My parents had given me permission to travel with the band director to pick up his car. Of course, I never told my parents the speed we drove. If my mother went ballistic over my rolling through a stop sign, I can't even begin to imagine what her response to that life-threatening speed might have been.

Even in young adulthood and after college, there was some level of rationale associated with my propensity to drive fast. I learned via word of mouth that if you received a traffic ticket, you could take defensive driving and have the ticket removed from your record.

What I didn't know at the time, but subsequently discovered, is that there is a cap on how much over the speed limit you can be traveling. If your speed is in excess of twenty-five miles an hour over the speed limit, a defensive driving class cannot be used in lieu of a ticket. I guess you could say I learned my lesson the hard way.

When I received my first traffic ticket for speeding, my wife subsequently opted to go shopping. She was intent on spending the same amount shopping for something tangible as I paid the court for my ticket. I guess you could say it was an expensive lesson learned. She was a lot more reserved than my mother had been when I received my first traffic ticket, but it was clear that she, too, found my behavior unacceptable.

Surprisingly, despite the adrenaline rush associated to speed, I have never had a desire to parachute out of an airplane. I am sure the concept of free falling would resonate with my spirit of adventure and the adrenaline rush would be over the top, but I am cautious enough that I want some kind of guarantee that eventually the parachute will open.

When my twin brother was stationed in Pensacola, Florida, for pilot training with the United States Marine Corps, he was required to parachute out of a plane several different times. On more than one occasion, they jumped out over the ocean. The stories he shared related to those experiences didn't make me think the adventure was that inviting.

In the mid 1970s, I was fascinated by the book *Zen and the Art of Motorcycle Maintenance*. It is the story of a father and son who traveled across the country from Minnesota to California on a motorcycle. There was something about the account of their jour-

ney that resonated with my spirit. It may have been the close connection between the father and son, the philosophical discussions
regarding the meaning of life or the simple thrill of experiencing
life firsthand, close to nature, and absorbing all of the outdoors
in your pursuit. It was awesome! I couldn't put the book down. I
found myself wanting to live that way.

There is something about fully experiencing the outdoors,
being absorbed in the beauty of nature, experiencing the sensation of speed and feeling the wind blowing through your hair
that excites and energizes me. Perhaps that is why I knew from
my first snow skiing experience that I longed for more.

Snow skiing combines the sensation of speed, the tranquility
of being in beautiful surroundings, and a Rocky-Mountain high
kind of experience that is closely akin to being in a perfect world.
It really doesn't get any better than that.

About two months after my introduction to snow skiing, I
found that I longed to repeat the experience. I really wanted to
learn how to ski, and the thrill of the adventure was irresistible.
I opted to take three days of vacation and went to Colorado to
go skiing with a friend who lived there and skied every weekend
during the season.

After I returned to work following my three days away, my
administrative assistant mentioned that another employee had
asked, "What's going on with Don? Why do you think he has
suddenly taken up snow skiing?"

My first thought was closely akin to "Does she think I'm pas-
sively suicidal and that I am a kamikaze on skis?" I've joked for
years around the office that my wife tells me every morning to
"make it accidental and work-related." (If you didn't catch the
implication, "accidental and work-related" doubles the life insur-
ance money.)

"What's going on with Don?" Actually, it seemed like a
strange question to ask. Of course, as is my general nature, I had
a tongue-in-cheek response. I enthusiastically responded, "*Great*

question! That is a really *great question!*" I think my voice tone got progressively louder each time I said "great question."

"Tell her you asked me. Tell her I had a premonition. Tell her it finally occurred to me that life is short and I'm getting old. Tell her if I don't take up skiing now, in all likelihood, I won't be able to take it up later. Tell her there are many assisted living programs with a chair lift, but they don't generally drop you off on a ski slope."

Have you ever wondered how your life would be different if you knew the future?

How many times have you said to yourself, "If I had known then what I know now?" If your retirement account is tied to the stock market, you've probably said that more than once. "If I had known then what I know now," I'd have invested more wisely.

If I had the insight to anticipate what lay ahead, I'd avoid any number of choices that subsequently proved to be less than desirable. Who wouldn't want the reputation of being a wise investor?

What about time management? I don't want to be relegated to a life of boredom. I want adventure. I want accomplishment. I want to know that I used every ounce of energy I've been given to pursue my dreams and to experience life fully. I don't want my final theme song to ever be "Is That All There Is?"

The writer of the book of James cautions us to avoid the mistake of making presumptions concerning the future. "Now listen, you who say, 'Today or tomorrow we will go to this or that city, spend a year there, carry on business and make money'" (James 4:13).

At times, we all do it. We are inclined to think our status quo is guaranteed for life. We think we have endless years and opportunities before us. Across the years, I've seen too many people who dropped out of the game and found it easier to observe life rather than experience life. I don't want to be a "couch potato" and live my life in an easy chair.

I want to connect with others. I want to have a sense of purpose. I want to find satisfaction in my work. I want life to be an adventure. I want life to be something other than a spectator sport. I didn't make the Little League baseball team, but I have subsequently discovered there are a lot of things I can do that bring enjoyment and satisfaction. I don't want to forfeit the opportunity to live life.

I was one of three speakers at my high school graduation in 1965. Somewhere tucked away in a filing cabinet, I still have the notes from that speech. They were typed on a standard Remington typewriter that belonged to my mother. (It was not an electric typewriter.)

At my high school, there was competition related to who was chosen to speak at graduation. Despite the fact that I was mostly terrified at the thought of public speaking, I opted to try out. I was chosen by a panel consisting of three high school English teachers to be included in the commencement program. That was true despite the fact that:

- I was not the class valedictorian or salutatorian;
- I was not selected by the student body as one of the top ten seniors to succeed. (My twin brother was; I wasn't.) We were pretty competitive. I was happy for him, but wondered why I was not selected;
- I never played football in high school;
- I never made the school basketball team. (I did try out in junior high. Sadly, I couldn't dribble the basketball and walk at the same time);
- It would take some thought, but I could probably come up with a list of recognitions that I didn't receive in high school;

- I did have some honors classes and an abundance of friends and I attempted to make every day an adventure filled with laughter and fun;

- I guess I can also say, tongue in cheek, I got in the last word. I was one of the commencement speakers at our high school graduation.

Several years ago, a colleague at work encouraged me to sign up on Facebook. Almost immediately, I concluded it was a mistake. I told my daughter and niece that I had joined Facebook. They both thought it was weird and said they had no interest in joining. I sent out several invitations to friends I seldom see. It took almost forever to find a handful of friends that were willing to connect with me on Facebook (I was beginning to think I'd never have enough for pallbearers—you need six friends for that).

However, within a few months, I reconnected with several friends from college, many of whom I haven't seen in forty years. I've also reconnected with a lot of friends from high school. For the ones who've been bold enough to post a picture on Facebook, I've got to tell you, "They look old!" Without exception, no one's life has turned out according to earlier plans.

Do you remember the song made famous by the Statler Brothers entitled "The Class of Fifty-Seven"?

> Tommy's sellin' used cars,
> Nancy's fixin' hair,
> Harvey runs a groc'ry store
> And Marg'ret doesn't' care;
> Jerry drives a truck for Sears
> And Charlotte's on the make,
> And Paul sells life insurance
> And part-time real estate.
>
> And the class of fifty-seven had its dreams.
> But we all thought we'd change the world
> With our great works and deeds;

Or maybe we just thought
The world would change to fit our needs.
The class of fifty-seven had its dreams.

Betty runs a trailer park,
Jan sells Tupperware,
Randy's in an insane ward,
And Mary's on welfare;
Charley took a job with Ford,
Joe took Freddy's wife,
Charlotte took a millionaire,
And Freddy took his life.

And the class of Fifty-Seven had its dreams
But livin' life from day to day
Is never like it seems.
Things get complicated
When you get past eighteen,
But the Class of Fifty-Seven had its dreams.
Ah, the Class of Fifty-Seven had its dreams.

Isn't it easy to make presumptions about the future? Life generally doesn't turn out the way we anticipate or expect. Despite our lofty goals as adolescents and young adults, we generally live ordinary lives.

It is only as we make ourselves available for the divine appointments God has for us that we can redeem the time and make investments with lasting significance.

James captures the essence of time when he says, "If it is the Lord's will, we will live and do this or that" (James 4:15). Let me remind you of Proverbs 3:5–6, "Trust in the Lord with all your heart and lean not on your own understanding; in all thy ways submit to him, and he will make your paths straight." That is the only way to successfully negotiate time management. When we approach life from that perspective, it really is more than enough.

LAID-BACK AND EASYGOING

I HAVE A tendency to think of myself as laid-back, easygoing, patient, and consistently kind. Relationally, I believe there is a win-win in every set of circumstances. While I generally have an opinion on how I want things done, it doesn't have to exclusively be done my way.

I may be wrong, but I think I'm pretty consistent in that approach. Tough on issues, easy on people. If anyone wants to suggest that I am "as solid as the rock of Gibraltar," I'll accept that as a fair assessment. I generally have a great rapport with others, and I attempt to be sensitive to their needs.

Don't we all see ourselves as that way? Our level of self-awareness related to our strengths and abilities can become pretty convoluted. We are reluctant to recognize the downside of our humanity.

"Laid-back, easy-going, patient, and consistently kind" are probably not the words that my wife would intuitively choose if she were going to paint a word picture of my character. For me even to suggest such a thing could cause anyone who knows me very well to wonder if my self-disclosure was more closely akin to a psychotic episode than a reflection of reality.

I was in Washington, DC, the majority of the second week in January 2013. My flight home was at 5:25 p.m. on Friday afternoon. Did I mention that I hate flying anywhere on a Friday afternoon? At that time of day, the airport becomes a quagmire of people all wanting to get somewhere quickly, and it mostly proves to be an environment of frustration.

- Surprisingly, under the category of good news, the plane boarded on time.

- Perhaps under the category of bad news, the flight was completely full. There was not an open seat on the plane.

- Let me bump that up a notch, under the category of really bad news, the man who took the middle seat on the row where I was seated needed a lot more space than was available in any of the seats.

To add insult to injury, after the doors of the plane were shut and an announcement was made to turn off all electronic devices, the plane didn't move away from the boarding ramp. We just sat there motionless.

After a few minutes of observing the passengers closest to me, I noticed the guy across the aisle and two rows up still had his iPad turned on. I found myself wanting to gently remind him that his iPad fell into the category of electronic devices.

The thing I found most frustrating was that people kept getting out of their seats and making their way to the front of the plane to use the restroom. As soon as one person returned to their seat, within seconds, someone else made their way to the front of the plane. This went on for about thirty minutes without any word of instruction or information from personnel on the plane. I was really beginning to get irritated.

Laid-back, easygoing, patient—probably weren't the best descriptors of my state of mind. I wanted to get on the airplane's intercom and remind people that everyone knew what time we were scheduled to leave and they should have taken care of business before they boarded the plane. Stay in your seats!

As I was fantasizing what I wanted to communicate to a plane full of people, I heard the pilot's voice coming through the intercom. He made the announcement that there was a problem with the restroom in the back of the plane and that we were waiting on maintenance personnel to arrive in order to fix the problem.

Oh great! How long do we have to wait for a plumber? "Easygoing, laid-back, patient—sure that defined me in that moment.

I even found myself getting a little irritated with the folks across the aisle. The two-year-old buckled in the middle seat didn't like the confinement. He was crying. After giving it some thought, I decided not to let that be annoying. After all, the child was only two; I could give him a break. At least I'm not totally hopeless.

Did I mention that the plane sat in the same position for the next hour?

At some point, I reached under the seat in front of me for my backpack and took out Max Lucado's book entitled *Grace: More Than We Deserve Greater Than We Imagine*. The very title of the book was convicting.

I was grateful the passenger sitting next to me didn't have the ability to read my mind. I would have been embarrassed holding a book entitled "grace" after the negative thoughts I'd been having. I had not mentally been at a place where grace had any part in my assessment of the endless number of people who I initially credited with the plane's delayed departure because they were out of their seats.

I turned to the page in the book where I previously left off. Its message was powerful: "To accept grace is to accept the vow to give it."

In one of his books, John Ortberg suggests, "God is closer than you think." He asks the hard questions:

- "If God is always with us, why is he so hard to find?"
- "If the Lord says his sheep know his voice, why doesn't he talk to you?"
- "If he's as relational as the Bible says he is, where's the intimacy?"

I have the wonderful privilege of working for a faith-based agency, but at times, I have the passing thought that it would work better if we were more faith-based. Sometimes there is a significant difference between what we articulate we believe and how those beliefs play out in the expression of our humanity. Our casework and counseling staff are highly trained and skilled professionals who have the ability to come alongside children and families in crisis and assist them in resolving conflict, solving problems, and moving into a more harmonious relationship.

Yet sadly, on more than one occasion, I've overheard staff members make reference to the level of family dysfunction they experience in their own lives and their seeming lack of concern or ability to orchestrate a different outcome.

It doesn't make sense to me. Can anything have a higher level of importance than the family ties and heritage we have been given? Truthfully, the only thing that is eternal in our lives are the people we are called to love.

Ortberg says "The story of the Bible isn't primarily about the desire of people to be with God; it's the desire of God to be with people."

A couple of weeks after my youngest grandson was born, we eagerly made our way to Northern California to spend time with our son and his family. It is not often that I journal my thoughts, but shortly after we returned home, I found myself wanting to share more time with my grandchildren. I wrote, "The two weeks since we were with our grandchildren feels more like two years than two fleeting weeks. During that time, Jake has doubled in age. Jenna is only five and William is three. Are they going through relationship withdrawal as well? Do they need to spend more time with Granddad?"

I longed to hold little Jake and rock him to sleep. I wanted him to know that he is loved by his granddad. After all, he was only two weeks old when we were in California. Now he is twice that age.

I find myself wanting to spend time with Jenna and William and simply share in whatever they enjoy doing. When we were there, William asked me to read a book to him. When I finished he said, "Read it again, Granddad. Read it again." I think I read the book four times before I convinced him to let me read something else.

My son and/or daughter-in-law generally initiate a telephone call to us at least weekly. Without exception, every time they call, we always ask, "Do the kids want to talk?"

Sometimes they do. There are times it is difficult to get off the phone with them. Sometimes Jenna, William, or Jake will want me to make up a silly song to sing to them. It's always awkward and a little embarrassing. I have this fear that one of the parents is also listening to my silly songs. As a rule of thumb, I tell the grandchildren frequently that it is okay to say that granddad is "crazy" as long as you say "crazy and fun."

Yet oftentimes, when we ask if the kids want to talk, they don't. They are busily involved in other activities. When they don't want to talk, that does not mean that we are not important or that they don't love us. It simply means they are preoccupied with activity.

Don't we do the same thing with God? When he reaches out to us, our attention is diverted and we don't want to talk. We are busy with other things.

Perhaps the best thing we can do is simply "be still, and know that I am [he is] God" (Psalm 46:10).

Our ability to discern our connection and relationship with God is often not intact. We don't always understand the reality of our circumstances.

These notes were recorded in my journal of random thoughts about a decade ago. The light was flashing on the answering machine. I had been outside doing yard work and had apparently missed someone's call. My first inclination was to wait until morning to check the machine. I was tired and dirty and didn't want to have to deal with anything else that day.

On the other hand, I have yet to ignore or defer checking a telephone message to the next day. Almost reluctantly, I pushed the button. I was relieved when I heard my son's voice. He said simply, "Dad I've got an important question for you. Becky and I have two different perceptions and only you can resolve the question for us. Please give me a call."

Knowing they were two hours behind us in time sequence, I immediately dialed his number. Hearing my voice, he quickly said, "Thanks for returning my call. I've got an important question for you. Would you describe yourself as a conservative?"

I responded, "I don't know how to answer your question. I guess it all depends on where I am. If I'm in the Austin area, I'd say I am very conservative. If I'm in Midland, I would describe myself differently." I jokingly tell people that when we lived in Midland you couldn't even make a left turn in traffic.

I also suggested to Craig that you can't stereotype or categorize people. It isn't true in every case, but "conservatives" are not thought as being very empathetic regarding social issues. I don't think of them as giving much thought to the plight of the poor, the needs of the elderly, or issues related to children's services. More often than not, economic issues and tax breaks for big companies take priority over the "little guy."

Craig explained that he and his wife were discussing her work as a child protective services caseworker, and she stated in passing that her boss wasn't a very good match of the agency where she worked because he was "too conservative." Craig countered that his dad was conservative and he thought I was a perfect fit for that kind of work. Becky laughed and told him he didn't know me very well if he would describe me as a "conservative."

Wanting to help Craig save face, I told him to tell Becky that if I am in West Texas, she is correct. No one in that venue would think of me as conservative. On the other hand, if I am in Austin, conservative might fit. I hung up the phone thinking about how differently Craig and Becky assess my value system. I was more content to think of myself as having empathy and a level of compassion for those in need.

A couple of days later, as I drove across Austin, at three separate intersections, I found myself stopped at traffic lights with folks holding signs that read, "Hungry, Need a Helping Hand." In each instance, I busied myself with adjusting the radio and purposefully paid very little attention to those standing outside in the heat looking for a handout. It was not until after I drove away from the third stoplight that I realized I had seen people standing on the street corner needing help, but I had not really seen them. How dare I be critical of folks I'd stereotyped as not having a lot of empathy for those in need? Had I not vividly displayed the same lack of empathy I'd ascribed to others?

The words recorded in the gospel of Matthew haunted me: "Then the righteous will answer him, 'Lord, when did we see you hungry and feed you, or thirsty and give you something to drink? When did we see you a stranger and invite you in, or needing clothes and clothe you? When did we see you sick or in prison and go to visit you?" (Matthew 25:37–39).

"The King will reply, 'Truly I tell you, whatever you did for one of the least of these brothers and sisters of mine, you did for me" (Matthew 25:40).

Sadly, my self-assessment is not always accurate. While I would be quick to describe myself as "laid-back and easygoing," there are times that I present myself very differently. I can be impatient with others. As a rule of thumb, it works best for me when things and plans go according to my schedule. It probably is magical thinking, but I also think of myself as empathic and compassionate. In contrast, the people standing on the street corner holding the signs that read "Hungry: Need a Helping Hand" would probably describe me otherwise.

Aren't we also told in scripture, "Therefore if anyone is in Christ, he is a new creation; the old has gone, the new has come!" (2 Corinthians 5:17). The reality is "Christ in you, the hope of glory" (Colossians 1:27) is the only hope that I have. When we approach life from that perspective, it really is more than enough.

AN EXAGGERATED SENSE
OF SELF-WORTH

SELF-DISCOVERY CAN BE a disturbing process. No doubt all of us have met people we've quickly assessed as having an overly exaggerated sense of self-importance. As a rule of thumb, I generally prefer to forego the experience of being in close proximity to folks manifesting a "the world turns around me" personification. Certainly that attitude could never be descriptive of my human pilgrimage. After all, I detest those types.

Shortly after beginning work for my current employer, a former employer involved in a pending lawsuit notified me that the attorney for the plaintiff had placed my name on a witness list. Consequently, my appearance was being requested for a deposition that would be videotaped.

As I reflected on the prospect of the deposition, I smiled to myself as I thought about how competent, professional, and responsible the agency would look based on the information I had to share. If I was sure of anything, it was that the plaintiff's attorneys would regret that my name had been added to the subpoena list. My testimony would not help their cause.

In addition, I took the opportunity to get a haircut and to have my beard trimmed. Image is important. Didn't I read somewhere once that clothes and appearance make the man? Although I am too old to personify that "young executive look," I could at least be a contender for honorable mention.

Because of my early morning deposition time, I drove to Dallas the evening before. I took my best suit, doubly starched white shirt, and a new tie. I was going to look good. It was quite a contrast to the laid-back, casual clothing I chose for the commute to Dallas. The slacks I wore probably had never seen an iron. They looked like something a "cedar chopper" would wear while working with a chainsaw or an axe. It was irrelevant; no one would see me before I arrived at the attorney's office at 8:15 a.m. the following morning.

I awakened the morning of the deposition long before the wake-up call I'd requested at the hotel. Truthfully, I was a little anxious. Okay, so I was more than a little anxious. I had not had an opportunity to review any documents or revisit any of the issues related to the deposition. I was left to the framework of my own memory. The circumstances around which I would be questioned had taken place nearly three years before. A review of documents would really have been helpful. Much of my earlier self-confidence was eroding.

By 6:00 a.m., I determined to get a head start on the day. Since I couldn't sleep, I might as well get dressed and head for an early breakfast. I was startled beyond imagination when I reached into the closet area to get my suit and discovered that the suit-trousers were not hanging with the suit-coat. There wasn't a variety of other choices to look through. The hanger containing my suit jacket and the hanger holding my shirt represented the totality of what was hanging in the closet. I closed the closet door, walked back into the bedroom area, and returned to the closet to look again. I don't know what I was thinking.

My taking a second look made me a candidate for some type of mental-health screening. What was I thinking? If the slacks weren't there the first time, it didn't take a Rhodes scholar to conclude they wouldn't be there later. This couldn't be happening! My trousers were not with the suit.

I don't know what I anticipated unless it was empathy, but I telephoned my wife to make her aware of my plight. She moved immediately into a "When are you ever going to learn?" lecture that added to my frustration and provided absolutely no comfort.

The die was cast. There was nothing I could do. I had no alternative but to wear the "cedar chopper" slacks I'd worn the day before. It was awkward! Instead of looking like the epitome of professionalism, my appearance was more closely akin to Bozo the Clown.

Before the morning concluded, my physical appearance was the least of my concern. The old Hebrew expression: "They ate my sack lunch" was fairly reflective of my interpretation of the tough questions and opinions they solicited. "Competent, professional, responsible" may not have been the descriptors that came to mind before the deposition was completed.

I was greatly humbled through the process. But then again, didn't I read somewhere that "pride goes before destruction" (Proverbs 16:18)?

Later, in reflecting on the experience, the Lord reminded me that my calling is to glorify him rather than myself. How could I have been so wrong? Obviously the primary difference between my behavior and that of others I detest as self-serving is only my inability to fairly evaluate all the attributes of my humanity.

Don't we all subsequently discover that "low man on the totem pole" is a very difficult task to negotiate? A great musician once said the most difficult chair in any orchestra is that of second chair. There is something inherently human about wanting to be in a position where our clout and influence is without question. We want to present ourselves as knowledgeable and influential.

Several years ago, at a reunion of extended family members, my mother was reminiscing about my childhood years. She made the observation that I got into more trouble than either of my brothers because I always insisted on having the "last word." I was a "yes, but…" kid. I always felt obligated to provide my side of the story even if it was unwanted or unmerited. Unfortunately, my mother was not willing to deter the "last word" to one of her children. Consequently, I received more spankings than both of my brothers combined. When my mother said, "I don't want to hear another word," she was intent with her expectations. I just didn't know when to be quiet.

Obviously, some things don't change. Interested in her reflection of my childhood years, with tongue in cheek, I told her one of my goals in life continues to be getting in the "last word." I reminded her that I normally am the one selected to officiate at family funerals. "Finally," I said, "I've found a forum where I can get in the last word and no one seems to mind."

Seriously, the bottom line is that most of us want to be in a position of power and control where we don't have to defer to the wishes of others. Isn't one of the common characteristics most of us experience the desire to "call the shots," make choices, give orders, provide leadership, and ensure that our wishes are carried out?

My wife would probably tell you that I am intent on having it done my way. Of course, I'd be quick to counter that is simply "projection" on her part. She, too, wants things done her way. While I don't concur that "doing it my way" is always my reality, I can easily concur that it is usually my intent. What's true of me is probably true of most of us.

Perhaps it was a similar mind-set that served as a baseline for the episode of betrayal and distrust that surfaced in the life of Judas Iscariot. Have you ever wondered what motivated a loyal trusted follower of Christ to turn on his mentor and friend?

Perhaps it was his intent to have Christ follow his directive rather than that of the Father.

Anytime we want it done our way instead of his way, we, too, place ourselves at risk to make the same disheartening discovery. For too much of my life, I have easily fallen into the category of self-promotion rather than "low man on the totem pole."

It would probably take months of therapy to fully understand my inherent need to be seen as credible and competent. Who's to say? Don't we all want to fit in and be an integral part of the team? The childhood scars associated with not being selected for the First State Bank Little League team at the age of nine may follow me to my grave. Consequently I continue to be very protective of my self-image when it comes to any kind of criticism or indication that my skill set might not meet expectations.

I still remember an awkward moment I experienced at a professional meeting several years ago. The meeting had just started and the chairman, a long-term friend, was saying, "I'm going to pass around a picture to see if any of you can identify the man on the left." It was an awkward moment because I intuitively had this fear that somehow I was going to be the brunt of the joke. Truthfully, the room was filled with people I hardly knew. I hoped against hope that I wasn't going to be the person depicted in the picture.

The people passing the photo around the table were looking briefly, shaking their heads from side to side expressing through their body language that they didn't recognize the person and passing the photo on to the person on their left. When the picture was finally in my hand, it only took a moment to realize my hope was short-lived.

The photo depicted four people. You guessed it. I was the guy on the left. The other three people were peers I previously worked with during my early years in residential child care licensing. I hadn't thought of them in years. The picture was probably taken at least thirty-two years before.

The word "geek" doesn't even begin to comprehensively describe the way the guy on the left looked.

The man in the photograph didn't appear to have ears. Or at least if he did, they were covered with long, dark brown hair. In addition, the man in the picture didn't have a beard. I've worn one since 1976. Hope was beginning to be rekindled that the photograph would escape recognition. Besides that, I can't remember when my hair was brown. I think it has always been gray. I would never have worn face-long sideburns and a mustache that looked like something out of a Wild West movie. I was even beginning to convince myself that it wasn't me.

The worst part was the clothing! Where did that awful looking shirt come from? This had to be a bad dream. I couldn't be seeing what I was seeing.

As the photo continued to be passed around the table, I managed to renew hope that I would escape recognition. After all, the person in the photo did not even come close to resembling the person that stares back at me in the mirror each morning. Perhaps I was safe.

No such luck. Someone on the other side of the room said, "It has to be Dan, but it doesn't look like him." My friend said, "Dan...do you mean Don?" And then there was laughter and several folks commented on the clothing.

After the laughter subsided and the meeting moved on to more substantive things, I managed to momentarily forget the photograph. Later in the day, I thought again about the picture and wondered what happened to the other three people pictured in the photo. At one time, we were work-related friends, but that all seemed like a lifetime ago.

And what about the strange-looking "geeky" guy on the left with the long hair and face-long sideburns? What became of him over the next three decades? Obviously I am still working in a related field; but professionally, relationally, and hopefully, even spiritually, I am not the same person.

The young man in the photograph had more quick answers and easy solutions than I can begin to muster today. I've learned through three additional decades of experience that life can be at times complicated and shades of gray make tough choices more difficult to process. In reality, life isn't all "black and white."

Easy answers and simple solutions don't stand the test of time. Life simply must be embraced with a dependency on the Lord and an abiding faith that, ultimately, he provides. Life is filled with far too many complications, quirks, challenges, losses, and difficulties to negate the need for his sovereignty and his grace.

Paul wrote, "For now we see only a reflection as in a mirror; then we shall see face to face. Now I know in part; then I shall know fully, even as I am fully known" (1 Corinthians 13:12). I have a better understanding today than I did three decades ago of the progressive nature of his disclosure and the ability to comprehend his grace. Hints of the comprehensive nature of his love have periodically altered any sense of self-sufficiency. The person who now looks back at me in the mirror is generally content for the experience to be on the journey.

Of course, from time to time, I still have a tendency to forget that it is not all about me. When I try to glorify myself rather than God, I always come up empty-handed. His power is made perfect in weakness. That really is more than enough.

NO REGRETS

IF I LISTEN to music in the car, I generally tune into satellite radio. I really like the opportunity to listen without commercials or interruptions. I recently drove my pickup to town. I'm still not sure how it happened, but the satellite station was tuned to a program entitled "Willie's Roadhouse."

The immediate sound caught me off guard. The sound of Jim Reeves was a flashback to forty years ago when I regularly listened to country music. Actually, it was so refreshing that I listened to the next couple of songs and really enjoyed the experience. I was beginning to think I had gravitated away from country music prematurely.

Then I heard a song that I'd never heard before. It was not a "feel good" song. The song was entitled "I'm the Only Hell (My Mama Ever Raised)." Interestingly, that was followed by "I Turned Twenty-one in Prison, Doing Life without Parole." I didn't hesitate. I turned the radio off and enjoyed the solitude of silence for the next few minutes.

Have you ever wondered how people find themselves in circumstances that destroy their lives? Do you just wake up one morning and tell yourself, "This is the day I am going to do something really stupid, and I'll spend the rest of my life paying for it?"

I have never had the misfortune of anyone telling me, "You have a right to remain silent. Anything you say can and will be used against you in a court of law." That would be commensurate with a death sentence for me, because God knows one of my needs is to have a voice. I'm not sure I could remain silent.

But what about less intrusive decisions that don't pose a threat for incarceration but leave us in the midst of broken relationships, high levels of stress, and a general dissatisfaction for the circumstances in which we find ourselves?

It was almost five years ago, but I have thought of the performance and the lyrics of the last song of the evening many times. We attended an 8:15 p.m. performance on a cruise ship in the Mediterranean. The entertainer was Brenda Cochrane, a vocalist from Scotland. I was mesmerized by the performance, particularly the last song.

She shared the story of Edith Piaf before she shared the song most associated with the singer, "Non, Je Ne Regrette Rien." Edith Piaf was the pride of France. She was said to hold the world in the palm of her hand. Without doubt, hers was a captivating voice. The love of Piaf's life was Marcel Cerdan, a boxer and former middleweight world champion. He was also married at the time. He died in a plane crash in October 1949 while flying from Paris to New York City to meet her. His death was the impetus for Edith's speedy decline further into the world of alcohol, drugs, and men.

Brenda Cochrane sang the song first in French and then in English. The English translation for the title is "No, I Have No Regrets."

> No, nothing at all, I regret nothing at all.
> Not the good, nor the bad. It is all the same.
> No, nothing at all, I have no regrets about anything.

It is paid, wiped away, forgotten.
I am not concerned with the past, with my memories.
I set fire to my pains and pleasures,
I don't need them anymore.
I have wiped away my loves and my troubles.
Swept them all away.
I am starting again from zero.

No, nothing at all, I have no regrets
Because from today, my life, my happiness, everything,
Starts with you.

The performance was so outstanding that we returned again for the 10:00 p.m. performance. The next morning, as we made our way to shore on one of the "tenders," Brenda was seated in the row behind us. Consequently, I had a chance to visit and tell her how much we enjoyed the performance. She seemed appreciative of the compliment and said that she really enjoyed being able to share the work and artistry of Edith Piaf.

What would it be like to live without regret? Aren't there times in each of our lives that we regret some of the decisions or choices that define a portion of our past?

- It may be a word spoken in anger.

- It may be something important that we failed to do.

- It may be the catalyst of pain that we orchestrated for someone else or for ourselves.

- It may be a harsh word spoken to a child.

The United States Department of the Treasury maintains a gift fund that was created in 1811. It was developed as an alternative for individuals to voluntarily repay the government for things stolen or defrauded. The first year it was established, only five dollars was received. During its first 175 years, over $5.7 million was contributed. Donations to the conscience fund vary in size:

- A nine-cent donation was made by a person from Massachusetts who had reused a three-cent stamp.

- A person from Jersey City sent forty thousand dollars in several installments for eight thousand dollars he had previously taken.

- Some donations are forwarded by clergy who have received deathbed confessions.

- Most donations are made anonymously.

- One person sent in a one-thousand-dollar cashier's check with the notation, "If I still can't sleep, I'll send you the balance."

I grew up in the "father knows best days" where the badge of successful parenting had something to do with one's children making it to adulthood without getting into too much trouble. My mother was intent to ensure no failure on their part. She was the primary disciplinarian in the family. I should know. I had lots of firsthand experience.

When spankings weren't effective and disciplinary issues still loomed, Mother always used God as the "trump card" to manage behavior. "If you really loved God you would… The Bible says…, etc." Of course, she was always right, but that was like taking out the big guns to swat a fly.

With the exception of the dynamite explosion at school, I never got into any real trouble that made the local or state news.

It is strange, but there are a couple of things from my childhood that surface on the conscious horizon of my memory from time to time. To some degree, it defies explanation.

I don't remember all the specifics; but my family along with aunts, uncles, and cousins were swimming in a location that had a beach. I think it was a lake near Fort Worth, but I may be mistaken. Some of the details aren't clear to me. At any rate, we brought with us some inner tubes to float on.

At one point, when we weren't using the inner tubes, another child from a different group asked if he could use one. I said, "Sure."

As he was taking the inner tube from our campsite to his, my uncle said to him, "Don't take that off."

The little boy responded, "He said I could take it," and pointed to me.

I don't know where the words came from, but I heard myself respond, "No, I didn't."

Maybe it has some relationship to the ongoing repeated pronouncement my mother made during my growing up years that "No liar would inherit the kingdom of Heaven," but sixty years later, I am still troubled by the memory.

When I was in elementary school, I had this ongoing fantasy that I was going to go to Colorado in search of uranium. It was really magical thinking on my part, but I believed it was possible. During that period of time, uranium findings in Colorado were televised on the news. I was always attempting to construct a soapbox car of sorts that I fantasized would be my method of transportation. Even as I write these words, I can only imagine how this information would have played out if anyone had ever administered a psychological evaluation. I would have been labeled for life.

One of the freedoms I had as a child was to roam around the immediate neighborhood or go the park that was a block away without the need for adult supervision. I always had to have permission, but there was not an issue related to personal safety.

One day, when I cut through a neighbor's yard taking a shortcut to the park, I found it. Miracle of miracles! I could tell from the shine and glimmer of the rock located in Mr. Voss's flowerbed that it was uranium. I didn't even think twice about it. I took it. Okay, I'll be honest, I stole it.

As luck would have it, our next-door neighbors had a Geiger counter. Mrs. Baker had the ability to confirm for me that the prize I held in my hand was indeed uranium. I lost no time knocking on her door and asking for her help. I was really disappointed when she confirmed the rock was not uranium.

I took the stolen rock and returned it to Mr. Voss's flowerbed. I also never made it to Colorado in my homemade soapbox, and I never discovered uranium. But from time to time, I painfully remember the details associated with these stories. I would be less than honest if I didn't tell you I find them bothersome.

I recently told someone that I have a couple of regrets related to parenting: one each with each of my children. Since they, too, were players in the experience, I will not share the details of our story. I'll simply say that I really lost my cool and I regret doing that. I wasn't physically abusive, but I wasn't calm and collected either. The memory is a source of pain knowing that I could have done it differently.

I also have regrets related to time management. I haven't always protected family time and kept it separate from work time. I also haven't balanced church time from extended family time.

Sometimes obligatory responsibilities color one's perception of expectations. Having had the privilege to pastor a church for over three and a half decades, it never occurred to me that Mother's Day was a time for adult children to purposefully return home to spend time with their mother. Despite the fact that adult children of parishioners were occasionally present at church on Mother's Day, I was oblivious to the notion that I could be slighting my mother by my failure to visit on that special day.

About ten years ago, my parents visited us over Mother's Day weekend. It made the day much more meaningful to share it personally with my mom. I sense she valued the time spent more highly than receipt of her Mother's Day gift or the Mother's Day card that I'd always sent in the past.

I even took the opportunity to share some "tongue-in-cheek" comments about my childhood during the church service. For example, I suggested the first Bible verse my mother taught me was the verse that said, "Be neat." I was almost grown before I discovered she made that part up. Of course, my mother could reference the commandment related to the need to honor one's father and mother. I stretched the truth a little bit when I suggested it was also one of the first verses she made me memorize.

I grew up in an environment where the ongoing expectation was you didn't do anything that could potentially bring embarrassment upon your family. I managed that pretty well through my childhood years. In my early adulthood, I moved to Austin and discovered a very different environment from the conservative West Texas town where I had been raised. When I first returned to West Texas for a family visit sporting a newly grown beard, my mother's first response was not, "Oh, Abraham Lincoln had a beard." It more closely resembled, "Charles Manson, the serial killer, has a beard."

From my mother's perception, my new look had the potential to bring disgrace to the family because responsible folks didn't wear beards. I decided since I didn't concur with her assessment, my failure to shave it at her request was not a purposeful violation of the commandment to honor one's mother.

Interestingly, from the vantage point of adulthood, the obligation to honor one's mother and father takes on an entirely different dimension. It evolved to the recognition of the need to provide a protective role in attempting to orchestrate decisions to promote their greatest good.

The need to honor one's father and mother isn't limited to one's childhood years. It really becomes a lifestyle that perhaps is more complex from the vantage point of adulthood. Failure for adult children to understand both the privilege and the responsibility to provide assistance to support the best interests of their parents is a fast track to the misery associated with regret.

My children are both grown. My son is forty-three and my daughter is thirty-three. Ours is a good relationship. We are really close, but I missed out on part of their lives because of work commitments.

If what is true for me is also true for you, please remember that doesn't negate the opportunity to be more attentive and supportive now. On the Father's Day weekend following Andrea's marriage to Kevin, they went to Dallas to visit with his dad. They did so with my well wishes and full support.

Knowing it was going to be Andrea's first Father's Day shared elsewhere, I found a really neat e-card and opted to send it to her. I quickly typed a note. It was from the heart, and it was genuine:

> Dear Andrea,
>
> There is something I've been meaning to say. I am so very proud of you. You have developed into a truly thoughtful, sensitive and kind person. I often marvel at the insight and thoughtfulness you display in your relationships with others. You are an incredibly supportive and loving aunt to Jenna, Lilian and William. You are so thoughtful in attending to the needs of your parents. Your life is extremely busy, but you take the time and initiative to communicate the value others add to your life.
>
> In addition, you display pride and high energy in your work environment. I can tell from our conversations that your employment is not just a job. It is an opportunity for you to use your talents and skill to enhance and make your company better.
>
> I am very proud of you!
>
> Love,
> Dad

What I wasn't prepared for was the response. I don't guess I even thought that a response would be forthcoming.

Later in the day, I received an e-mail that was very touching. It said,

> Wow, Dad, I am speechless. This is one of the most precious cards I have ever received. I will treasure it always.

Children learn what they live and you are truly an amazing example. I would say more, but I'm sitting here crying at work so I better end this for now.

I love you and will miss being with you on Sunday.

Love,
Your very proud daughter.

When we figure out a way to remove regret from our lives, it really does pay off in dividends. Under the Lord's leadership, it really is more than enough.

UNPRECEDENTED JOY

MY SON AND his wife were married for almost ten years before they had their first child. We were beginning to think we would never have grandchildren. They telephoned us on New Year's Eve 2002 to let us know we were going to be grandparents.

The words were music to our ears. As a chain reaction to the wonderful news, the following week became one of nostalgic contemplation as I thought of any number of things associated with being a grandparent. For starters, "What name will my grandson or granddaughter use to refer to me?"

That's a tough one. I have such wonderful memories of both sets of my grandparents that I intuitively knew I had a tall order to fill if I could ever hope to be as supportive, caring, and important in the life of my own grandchild. What a challenge!

As I eagerly gave myself permission to contemplate the new role I'd be assuming, I wondered if there was anything I'd do differently in fulfilling the role of granddad with my own grandchild when the time came. I didn't come up with much:

- I was saddened to realize that my grandchild will never know the joy of sitting in my lap and steering the car down the highway. (It just isn't safe.)

- My grandchild will miss the thrill of riding in the back of a pickup truck. He or she will not experience the adrenaline rush of standing in the back of the truck holding on to the headache rack while traveling down the road at sixty miles per hour. (Obviously, guardian angels were working overtime during my childhood.)

- My grandchild will miss the opportunity to play with fireworks on the fourth of July. (Since the dynamite cap explosion, I'm respectful and distant myself from explosives of any kind. It is safer that way and I definitely want to provide a safe environment for my grandchildren.)

Short of that, there is absolutely nothing else I resolved to change.

I remember going through that same exercise of thoughtful contemplation when it came to parenting. The list related to parenting was a little more substantive. For example:

- I promised myself that I would not put my children on guilt trips as a tool to manage their behavior.

- I promised that I'd give my children opportunity to fully articulate their position in resolving any kind of conflict.

- I promised myself that I would look for reasons to say "yes" rather than "no" when they wanted to go somewhere or do something.

- I promised myself that when they became adults and married, I'd never interfere with whatever holiday plans they made or how much time they spent with the other family.

Unfortunately, most of us have a tendency to parent in the very same fashion in which we were parented. Old tapes and previous life experiences have a tendency to color our perceptions and offer ready solutions. In looking at the parenting list I made, the only item I've successfully completed was the last one.

Prior to my oldest grandchild's birth, I asked my son, "What will you do differently as a parent from your perception of how you were parented?" It was almost without needing to give it any thought, he turned to me, smiled, and said, "I'm not saying it wasn't effective because it was, but there has to be a better way than manipulation through guilt." Ouch! Despite my best intent to play it out differently, old patterns are very difficult to leave behind.

When it comes to family, I have such a rich heritage. All of my grandparents lived to be at least ninety years of age. Their minds were engaging, their health was good, and they lived independently. They devoted themselves to cherishing the family and friends they had been provided.

I did not take any of it for granted even in the midst of adulthood. I have such treasured memories of time shared with my grandparents (childhood and adulthood). In addition to enriching my life they also enriched the lives of my children.

The close-knit experience on both sides of my extended family is atypical of many. I know of no other clan that maintains the closeness and sense of family support that we share together. Despite the closeness, we are not an enmeshed family. We maintain individual lives and attend to the needs of our immediate family. At the same time, we continue to share a special bond with extended family members. Across the years, we have shared intimately in fun times, family holidays, vacations, and weekend visits. We have also stood side-by-side in a spirit of solidarity through times wrought with great difficulty.

I know each of our family members maintain a treasure chest of individual and family memories, coveted times shared together, and a sense of closeness that continues despite circumstances or separation through death.

As an example, the following letter to my maternal grand-mother on her ninetieth birthday was intended to reinforce the value and enrichment she has brought to my life. I hand delivered it when I attended her birthday party. I subsequently wrote a similar letter to my paternal grandmother when she celebrated her ninetieth birthday. That, too, was hand-delivered.

Dear Grandma,

I consider myself fortunate to have the opportunity to share in the celebration of your 90th birthday. Few people my age are blessed with anything other than the memory of a grandmother's love, so I feel privileged to continue to share in that experience. Some of the fondest memories of my childhood relate to times we shared together; the summer vacations, holidays, and weekend visits.

I know that to a large degree the experiences of childhood are determinative in the values, lifestyle, and feelings of self-worth that accompany one's adulthood. With that in mind, I should have turned out better than I did. Few children have the opportunity to be as nurtured by two sets of grandparents as I did.

Interestingly in the midst of adulthood, I still find that I draw strength from your influence and the value that you give to life. I am taking the occasion of your 90th birthday to say thanks for the special person that you are.

In attempting to sort out my thoughts, I got real nostalgic and in my memory relived the experiences of the past. Through that process I shed tears of joy and sadness mingled together to validate that my assessment of your influence is correct.

To some degree the early years of my childhood blend into oblivion. The rambling old house at Ringgold is what comes to mind when I think of Grandma's house. This is true despite my memory of your also living in McCamey and in Conroe for a brief period of time.

From the vantage point of a child's perspective, the house in Ringgold was wonderful because it radiated with family times; uncles, aunts and cousins. Of course, you and Grandpa were always there. The wrap-around front porch with wooden railing was a great conversation place, particularly late at night in the company of cousins.

As a child, I envisioned the house at a significantly higher elevation than the road. It was a great place for playing cowboys and Indians and rolling down the hill. I was startled in adulthood to drive by the house and realize that the hill was little more than a slight incline.

Winter nights around Christmastime were the coldest to be found anywhere; unless of course you were lucky enough to get to sleep on the feather mattress in the small bedroom next to the dining room.

I am surprised with the details I still remember about that house, even down to the statuary dog that served as a door stop. With rare exceptions, the experiences to be found there were warm, fun, family times. I remember that Grandpa Long would give us a nickel to hug his neck. I also remember that you couldn't get within ten feet of the bathroom because it served as a conference site for the DeMoss girls. I still wonder about what or who they talked about in there.

There were wonderful experiences associated with life in that locality. You introduced me to new potatoes and gravy and insisted that we go to Vacation Bible School year after year. One summer you even invited the preacher and evangelist home for dinner. I'd never been that close to a preacher before, but those guys were really nice and it turned out okay. In fact, I'm still kind of partial to a small country church experience. I guess I have you to thank for that.

I could go on and on with the fun times, but let me throw in some negatives as well. On occasion we went with you to pick wild plums for jelly. That in itself was bad enough, but the chigger bites that followed caused agonizing anguish and seemed to itch for weeks. And then there was the time Ronnie and I got into trouble for sliding down the fire escape at the courthouse in Montague. As I remember it, you were not too happy with us.

Grandma, when I think of you, I think of strength, faith and love. No doubt it's from your faith that you find your strength. That combination has consistently worked for you. I have to admit that at times I'm a little envious; things aren't always that clear cut for me.

I know of few extended families that are as close knit as the DeMoss clan. I can't explain it apart from the influence that you have consistently imparted.

In late adolescence, I contemplated writing an article and attempting to have it published in Reader's Digest under the heading: "My Most Unforgettable Character." I wish now that I had followed through with that desire. Of course the subject matter would have been your strength/faith relationship.

My observation of the way you handled two tragic experiences were the source of my conclusion.

To a large degree my childhood was sheltered from sadness. The first time it really invaded my life in an overwhelming way related to the illness and subsequent death of Uncle Travis at the age of twenty-seven. From my perspective his death was unfair and God should have intervened. Yet I noticed that your faith did not falter, it seemed to grow stronger. You didn't retreat in bitterness and blame God, but encouraged Grandpa and the rest of your family as you worked through your own grief.

The second observation from which I sensed your strength related to the time your neck was broken in an automobile accident and the recovery period that followed. I can vividly remember the metal clamp and cable coming out of your head as you lay in traction. It was a very frightening experience to see one's Grandma in that shape. And then of course, there was that horrible cast subsequently placed over your head. It looked gruesome to me, but again you accepted it in stride, strength and faith never wavering.

All of that had a positive impact from a child's perspective. What I have since discovered, with no surprise, is that you have consistently taken that same approach to life. I can think of no situation where you haven't negotiated life with dignity and a steadfast faith. Hopefully someday I'll do a better job of adopting your approach.

Happy Birthday and thanks...

Love,
Don

I was thirty-six years old when my first grandparent died. Even today, the influence of my grandparents and the value they add to my life continues. If you walk through our home, you'll find an assortment of things they left behind. They have no monetary value, but they serve as a visual reminder that triggers my memory of their love and range of influence.

In every place we've lived since 1976, I have displayed a small shadowbox picture frame containing the gold pocket watch that belonged to my paternal grandfather. The frame also includes a picture of my paternal grandparents. When we moved to our current home ten years ago, the frame and watch automatically were included in a grouping of pictures on display in my study.

Granddad gave me the watch when we first moved to Austin in 1976. He had come for a visit and took the watch out of his pocket. He said he knew I'd always admired it and that he'd like for me to have it. I was speechless. I had it framed the following week. Incidentally, every time Granddad saw the watch displayed on a wall in our home, he'd caution me that someone was going to steal it. But that never happened.

My granddad lived to be ninety-six years of age. Consequently, I had the pocket watch in my possession seventeen years prior to his death and a total of twenty-six years since it was given to me.

Over the past seven to eight years prior to our moving to our current home, my son has mentioned on a number of occasions that when I'm finished with Granddad's watch, he'd really like to have it. He absolutely idolized my granddad. They had a very close relationship.

Just prior to the Christmas holidays, after moving into our home, I mentioned to my wife that I thought it was time to pass Granddad's pocket watch along to our son. Our home is filled with vivid reminders of my grandparents: old photographs, an assortment of old tools, crochet, a walking cane, and other items too numerous to mention. I could part with the watch and still have ample reminders of the influence and wonderful contributions my grandparents made to my life.

When my son and his family had a chance to get settled in our home for the holidays, unknown to me, my son asked his mom what I'd done with Granddad's watch. He noticed it was no longer on display. She simply responded that I'd put it away for safekeeping.

When I presented Craig with the watch late on Christmas afternoon, he got teary-eyed, I got teary-eyed, and we both spent a few moments of silence remembering the wonderful contributions Granddad made to both of our lives.

On June 16, 2011, my wife and I had the wonderful privilege of attending the award ceremony where our son was awarded the Bronze Star for his military service in Afghanistan. The ceremony turned out to be much more than I expected. Throughout the course of meeting lots of folks, including the colonel who made the presentation, it was clear that Craig is highly regarded and valued as a leader and colleague. (Trust me, from a parent's perspective that was filled with feel-good moments.)

Craig's comments after the colonel had spoken caught me totally off-guard. You would have thought he'd done public speaking as a career track. He was articulate and commanding in his address:

- He first recognized the outstanding level of love and support he shares and experiences with Becky, his wife. He said her commitment to being an exceptional wife and mother provided all the assurance he needed to free him to focus primarily on doing his job.

- Craig also made some very nice comments related to his family and the values carried over from childhood (I had to fight the inclination to get teary-eyed.)

- He shared credit for receipt of the Bronze Star with the entire team that worked with him. He could not have been more complimentary of those who worked alongside him. "It was the most capable group of men I have ever had the privilege of serving alongside."

- Lastly, he thanked the colonel for creating the kind of environment that made team members want to do their best. Reportedly, the experience for him had been filled with teaching moments, and the assignment was something he highly valued. He said he didn't know how his work environment could get any better than what it has already been.

We were pleased to have the opportunity to be present for the ceremony and to spend time with grandchildren.

One of the things I also observed while visiting in their home is how taxing and difficult it can be to be a parent. At the time, Craig had a seven-year-old, six-year-old, and two-year-old. They are mostly precious children. (Heavy emphasis on "mostly.") Trust me, they can periodically pose a challenge or two unless, of course, you are used to "bloodcurdling screams" and declarations of war. Honestly, I had the passing thought, "Will they make it to adulthood without killing one another?"

Actually, at one point, even the two-year-old bit my thumb. I almost let out a bloodcurdling scream myself. I thought a great white shark had attacked me. Of course, when Jake, the two-year-old, saw the look of terror and pain on my face, he was delighted.

The thing I noticed is that Craig didn't get overly rattled by any of it. His priority is his kids; and with the "patience of Job" kind of approach, he provided structure, redirection, and individual attention and support. It was all such a contrast to how I suspect he manages himself at work (or maybe not). At any rate, it was effective. It made me proud to be a dad and grandfather.

The wonderfully rich heritage and legacy I've been provided by loving grandparents has set the bar for the kind of grandparent I want to be. I tell my grandchildren every time I share time with them that it is okay to say that Granddad is "crazy" as long as they say I am "crazy and fun." I want to create wonderful memories for them. It really is more than enough.

KINDNESS AND GRATITUDE

I MADE THE flight reservation six weeks earlier. When the day actually arrived, I was filled with anticipation. As I boarded the plane, I envisioned that Denver would resemble a winter wonderland. Disappointingly, when the plane landed, that proved not to be the case. Looking out of the window of the airplane, there was not a visible patch of snow on the ground or any evidence of a snowflake in the air. I really had envisioned something quite different. I felt part of the elation I experienced earlier begin to deflate.

The plane landed about an hour and a half before the end of the workday. I was being picked up by a friend who lives in Denver as soon as he got off work. Knowing there would be a delay, I was content to sit in the waiting area and read a book for what I anticipated would be about an hour and a half.

At some point, when I looked up from my reading, I noticed in my peripheral vision that snow was falling outside. It immediately energized my spirits. Actually, in short order, a lot of snow was falling in Denver.

Lost in thought regarding the snow and envisioning skiing on fresh powder, I immediately fantasized the level of enjoyment the experience would hold. I had the good fortune of skiing under those conditions the last time I was in Denver. The sound of my cell phone notifying me of a text message brought me back to the here and now. The text stated simply, "Traffic is horrible. Nothing is moving." What should have been a twenty-minute commute for my friend picking me up at the airport proved to take an hour and a half.

When he finally arrived, he told me it was good I had flown in early. He had just heard on the news that other flights scheduled to arrive in the evening had been cancelled due to the amount of snow.

As we slowly made our way around the outskirts of Denver toward the mountains to the west, the news broadcast on the radio focused on the immobilization of Denver by the first heavy snow of the year. At the time of the report, the traffic in the city was barely moving and eight inches of snow was predicted by nightfall.

It had been two years since my last trip to the ski resort west of Denver. It was good to be back. Needless to say, it was way past the dinner hour when we arrived at our destination, and I was grateful the restaurant was still open. Sitting across the table from my friend and enjoying the opportunity to visit underscored for me how incredibly fortunate I have been to be the recipient of his friendship. Regardless of the lapse of time between opportunities to visit, it always seems like it was the day before yesterday, and we pick up again where we left off. It is a very comfortable experience.

We have little in common other than having been neighbors in Dallas. Our ongoing friendship is forged out of that experience. He has lived in Denver for the past several years. Following my initial and immediate obsession with skiing, he issued an open invitation to come to Denver anytime I wanted to ski. He works in the high-tech industry and has a pretty flexible work schedule. Somehow he manages to find time to devote almost every weekend of the ski season to skiing. He is an exceptional skier and intuitively knows I need all the help I can get.

Perhaps he knows I am at risk unless someone provides structure and parameters around my downhill experiences. His initial assessment of my skill set probably has remained unchanged since the first time he saw me ski. Although he is always thoughtfully encouraging and acknowledges that I'm making great progress, he thinks I ski way too fast to ensure my personal safety and the safety of others on the slopes with me.

Every time I've come to ski, he has shared his belief that I should devote a day of skiing under the watchful supervision of a professional ski instructor. He maintains that is the best way to increase my skill set and learn to navigate safely down the mountain. How do I argue with that? I jokingly have told folks that my long-term goal in life is to become a ski instructor after I retire. Since I plan to continue to work for a very long time, perhaps I still have ample opportunity to learn. At any rate, I've taken a lesson each time I've skied in the Denver area, and I have observed that many of the instructors are well into their golden years. Perhaps there is hope for me.

The ski trip couldn't have been more perfect. The mountain resort was covered with fresh snow and snow continued to fall throughout the first day. The beauty of the resort was almost too much to fully process and comprehend. The purity of the freshly fallen snow, the lining of the ski runs with the splendor of pine trees and the majesty of the mountains all seemed in perfect accord. They echoed the statement that all was well with the world.

It all seemed like such a refreshing contrast to the world I left behind and the busyness and demands of a typical week. I was soaking up nature and the beauty of my surroundings instead of reading e-mail or attempting to complete a task on my never-ending "to do" list. I was also even communing with God and thankful for the totality of the experience.

By the end of the daylong ski lesson, I was feeling pretty confident. In uncharacteristic fashion, I had not fallen. The ski instructor was consistent in his praise and one of the other participants told me while we were riding the ski lift together that I skied really well. She even added that she didn't know why I was taking the class. I was feeling pretty confident and on top of my game as we made our final descent down the mountain. My confidence was higher than it has ever been. It had been a really good day!

The end was in sight, but the last decline was steep. I probably wasn't as focused as I should have been. I was obviously traveling at a faster rate of speed than I could control, and I ended the run falling down. The fall ruined my perfect record of the day, but it helped immensely in the area of enhancing my humility level. I wasn't "king of the mountain." I was simply a long-term novice who had really had a good day on the ski slopes. Life was good. I even smiled the next day when I heard an ad for a life-alert system indicating that one in three persons over the age of sixty-five falls down. You bet I did, but gratefully, I had no difficulty getting back up.

As the first day of skiing came to a close, before I drifted off that night in sleep, I asked God what I was supposed to learn from the incredible experiences of the day. As I reflected on the question, the answer I received surprised me. What clearly came to mind was that I needed to experience a higher level of gratitude. In essence, I needed to be more thankful.

The opportunity to ski in the Denver area is not an entitlement. It is a gift regularly provided by a long-term friend who voluntarily sets aside his regular routine and invests the time to ensure I enjoy the ski experience and navigate it safely. I am truly the recipient of his kindness. It is beyond my deserving.

He obviously takes delight in knowing he has orchestrated a venue for me that is rejuvenating and energizing. He selflessly puts his life on hold and devotes a couple of days one or two times a ski season to simply find enjoyment in providing me the opportunity to pursue my dreams and enjoy the challenges and thrills associated with the mountain. He is a kind and generous friend.

When you stop to consider it, isn't kindness the baseline for friendships? Earlier this year, I carried over a previous New Year's resolution to reconnect with some people who have contributed significantly to my life. I wanted to take the opportunity to reconnect and validate they have enriched my life greatly. Perhaps I've always needed to experience a higher level of gratitude and express a higher level of thankfulness.

Many of those on the list that I hope to reconnect with are friends from another place and another time. For whatever reason, I didn't invest the effort to stay connected. Most of those on my list live at other locations across the state and our paths don't have reason to connect unless there is purposeful intent on the part of one or the other.

Part of the driving force for my resolution is to ensure that I take the opportunity to affirm my gratitude for the gift of their friendship. I have been fortunate to be surrounded by capable and caring people. Friends have showered me with kindness, and it has enhanced my life greatly. I just need to do a better job of keeping up with them.

The need to keep up with them reminds me of a very awkward moment. Five or six years after we relocated back to the Austin area, my wife and I were walking through a department store. From across the room, I heard my name being called out. Looking up, I saw a woman and teenage girl walking in our direction. The woman looked familiar. It was obvious that she knew me and seemed delighted that our paths had crossed. For the life of me, I struggled to remember some clue as to her identity. My inability to glean even a hint regarding the setting in which I knew her was not only a source of embarrassment but also a basis of real concern. After all, what was wrong with my brain that I had no specific recollection? Something obviously was wrong.

She greeted me with a friendly hug and seemed genuinely pleased to run across us. In a panic, I quickly asked if she'd met my wife. She extended her hand and said, "Hello, I'm Cindy." She then introduced her daughter.

Despite the fact that the computer in my brain was processing the name Cindy over and over, nothing was registering. I simply drew a blank. Somewhere in my consciousness was the desire to ask for more identifying information. After all, if I could pin down where in the state I knew her from, it might render a clue regarding her identity. I knew that I knew her. I just couldn't place the setting. Consequently, I was at a loss to know what to say.

I almost asked if she was still living in Midland. After all, we had lived in Midland for twelve years. It seemed probable that I knew her from that locality. As I contemplated verbalizing the question, I opted to delete it from my repertoire for fear that this lady and her daughter had never been to Midland. After all, how awkward would that be for them if I was wrong regarding the location?

Instead I played it safe. It was almost as if the old familiar adage of "fake it till you make it" instinctively kicked into gear. I said something really innocuous like, "So good to see you again" and moved into a discussion of asking what they were hoping to accomplish on their shopping spree. To add to the conversation, I filled in the details of what we were hoping to find. We chatted briefly, expressed gratitude for the happenstance meeting, and moved on to complete our shopping.

I couldn't shake the name "Cindy" out of my mind. I knew it would get priority in my thought processes until the puzzle was solved.

Twenty minutes later and ten miles down the freeway, it hit me. Cindy had been an administrative assistant in the office where I'd worked over two decades before. Suddenly there were a hundred and one questions I wanted to ask her. I was both delighted and regretful that our paths had crossed. The regret had to do with the lost opportunity to really communicate. It would have been great to renew an old friendship and ask some pertinent questions regarding her current life circumstances.

If I had a clue regarding Cindy's current last name or information on how to contact her, I'd telephone in a heartbeat to apologize for the less than personal reception she received from me. I would have been delighted to renew the acquaintance.

I learned something about the merits of honesty over "faking it until you make it." If I'd had the courage to truthfully communicate that I needed help in recalling who she was and where I knew her from, Cindy would have filled in the puzzle, and I'd have had the opportunity to actually connect on a feeling level and renew an old friendship.

Instead, pride and subtle dishonesty were the catalysts that turned an opportunity into failure.

Going forward, I want to be a friend who values relationships. I want to be a friend who demonstrates kindness. I want to be the kind of friend who is willing to put my life on hold when an opportunity presents itself to be kind to someone else.

Some time ago, I received an e-mail message from a long-term friend who purchased a ranch in central Texas and moved from Dallas to the country. In providing an overview of the new place, she also included a description of her new pastor. It supports the notion that people respond positively to kindness. When people sense they are loved and supported, the connection that is forged is meaningful and fulfilling.

She wrote, "I like all my neighbors including the pastor of our church.

Truthfully, he is really no kind of preacher—couldn't preach his way out of a paper bag; however, he is a real pastor. He would help you get your truck out of a ditch, set up your deer feeder, take your grandma to the doctor, sit up with a sick relative, or help you fix your roof. He really cares about all the people around here, and he is so funny.

He has a great sense of humor. Last Sunday, he talked about his visit to the 'Bass Pro Shop' sports extravaganza in Grapevine, and you could tell it was a true religious experience for him…all that huntin' and fishin' equipment in one place. Anyway, I actually enjoy going to church, can you believe it?"

Kindness can make a long-term difference when shared to meet others at the point of need. How many people do you know who would help you get your truck out of a ditch, set up your deer feeder, take your grandma to the doctor, sit up with a sick relative, or help you fix your roof? I want to be that kind of friend. Don't you?

I like the way Christ expressed it:

> Then the King will say to those on his right, "Come, you who are blessed by my Father; take your inheritance, the kingdom prepared for you since the creation of the world. For I was hungry and you gave me something to eat, I was thirsty and you gave me something to drink, I was a stranger and you invited me in, I needed clothes and you clothed me, I was sick and you looked after me, I was in prison and you came to visit me."
>
> Then the righteous will answer him, "Lord, when did we see you hungry and feed you, or thirsty and give you something to drink? When did we see you a stranger and invite you in, or needing clothes and clothe you? When did we see you sick or in prison and go to visit you?"
>
> The King will reply, "I tell you the truth, whatever you did for one of the least of these brothers of mine, you did for me."
>
> Then he will say to those on his left, "Depart from me, you who are cursed, into the eternal fire prepared for the devil and his angels. For I was hungry and you gave me nothing to eat, I was thirsty and you gave me nothing to drink, I was a stranger and you did not invite me in, I

needed clothes and you did not clothe me, I was sick and in prison and you did not look after me."

They also will answer, "Lord, when did we see you hungry or thirsty or a stranger or needing clothes or sick or in prison, and did not help you?"

He will reply, "I tell you the truth, whatever you did not do for one of the least of these, you did not do for me." (Matthew 25:34–45)

There is absolutely no way to calculate or evaluate the difference our involvement (his involvement through us) can make in the lives of others who need our help. I'd like to be the kind of person who is always available to help others at the point of need. The short-term and long-term benefits of investing our lives in that regard have merit. With God in the mix, it is more than enough.

THE GIFT OF PAIN

THE INTENSITY AND emotions surrounding pain often diminish from memory as our circumstances change and life becomes more comfortable for us. At least that has been my experience. The truth of the matter is, we simply don't remember pain with the same level of intensity and sense of helplessness that often is associated with the initial experience. If this were not true, how could anyone ever traumatized by life find the resources to go on?

Over four decades ago, I went through a period of health-related difficulties that seemed potentially overwhelming at the time. Before the ordeal was over, I was under the care of three physicians; two internists and a neurologist. After several months of bizarre symptoms, two different hospitalizations, and scores of painful tests, one physician was adamant about labeling the illness. The second physician was 90 percent sure and the third opted for a "wait and see" approach before rendering a diagnosis. Consequently, it was with little effort that I gravitated toward the third physician as my primary caretaker. The choices provided by the first and second physicians were debilitating at best.

Fortunately, forty years later, I am enjoying exceptional health and am still in the "wait and see" mode. I highlight that experience only because it serves to substantiate how easy is it to disassociate one's memory from anything remotely associated with pain. The downside to that approach to living, however, is that some of the lessons learned during the process can also be minimized or forgotten as well.

With effort, I can force myself to reexamine some of those past experiences, but the intensity and emotions associated with that period of my life has mostly been buried in the recesses of my memory. However, two lessons learned (which sometimes become easily forgotten) immediately come to mind. Both relate to the resourcefulness of God.

I have never been one to ascribe to the "name it and claim it" theology that is prevalent with many today. From my perspective, if God can be reduced to a "genie in a bottle" to respond to our every wish and desire, then we ultimately become the power-brokers and God becomes the servant. I don't think that is what he meant when he talked about the importance of making our requests known to him. He assists us in identifying his will and making known our requests of him.

Shortly before the onset of a myriad of health problems that I experienced, God led me to pray for something that seemed fairly trivial at the time. In fact, I almost felt stupid bothering the Lord with my request but felt led to verbalize my petition anyway. He answered immediately. God subsequently used the reminder of that experience to bolster my faith when I needed the strength and support that only he could provide.

I've always had a tendency to be a little obsessive-compulsive in wanting things to look just right. My wife and I had purchased a home in Fort Worth. One of my first projects was to construct a privacy fence and screen around a portion of the patio area. When I finished the task, I had a fence-line of lumber, all three feet in length, left over.

It was a Saturday afternoon, and I compulsively placed all the leftover lumber neatly stacked at the edge of the driveway at the front of the house. Trash pickup wasn't scheduled until some time during the week, but that location was as good as any to dispose of the leftover lumber.

As I was placing the last board on the stack, I looked up and saw a station wagon coming down our street. For some strange reason, I felt led to pray, "Lord, let the people in that station wagon stop and ask for this lumber." It was a strange request. I was uncomfortable verbalizing that request, but I felt compelled to do so. I stood there not knowing what to think when the people in the station wagon drove past our home and turned left at the corner. I simply dismissed the prayer as wishful thinking on my part and went into the house.

It was a short time later when the doorbell rang. Answering the door, I was startled to see the station wagon parked next to our curb. The driver wanted to know if he could have the stack of wood.

It was a simple prayer. It was one that I would never have thought to ask on my own. In the months that followed, God reminded me repeatedly of his availability and strength. It was almost as if he was saying, "I've shown you I can handle the little things. Now trust me to handle the larger ones."

It was out of that experience that the second lesson I learned surfaced. It was on a Sunday morning. I was in church with my wife and two-year-old son. The offertory was being played, and I processed the words of the hymn almost as if I was hearing it for the first time, "Because He lives I can face tomorrow…" Suddenly, it became clear to me that the fears and anxiety I was experiencing related to thoughts of a debilitating illness were basically inconsequential. In the final analysis, my relationship with God through faith in Christ had already guaranteed the ultimate outcome. I was at peace with God, and that is all that virtually mattered. Everything else was window dressing.

I emerged from the experience of worship a little teary-eyed with a determination to simply trust God to provide the resources I needed to get through the day. If it all ended tomorrow, eternity was fixed and all was well with my soul. Long-term planning came to be associated with plans for the next weekend. I refused to consider life beyond a seven-day window frame.

It is incredible to discover how simplified life can become when we just focus on making the most of each day. Unfortunately, through the four decades that have come and gone since that time, I've lost that sense of imperative in focusing only on the now. I often find myself occupied with too full an agenda to accomplish in a single day. Consequently at times life becomes lost in living.

In reflecting back on that period of difficulty in my life, I have to acknowledge that coming to terms with my ultimate dependency upon him was worth the price of admission. I wish now that I had recorded the feelings, observations, and personal reflections associated with those experiences.

The writer of James suggests we ought to praise him for all things. In hindsight, at some level, I believe it is easier to do that "after the fact" than while in the midst of difficulty.

I remember two visitors from church who came by my hospital room to share words of encouragement. I had never met either of the men before and was somewhat taken back when they suggested, "I needed to thank God for what I was experiencing." It may have been sound advice, but I was not at a level physically or spiritually where words of gratitude would have been genuine. I did express a genuine prayer of thanksgiving for their departure after they left my hospital room.

From an experiential level, it was not until I discovered the resourcefulness of God as he spoke to me in the midst of an offertory hymn that I came to experience a sense of peace related to my circumstances. Truthfully, it was much later before I was in the "thank you" mode for the learning I experienced as a result of those circumstances.

I have to admit, if given a choice, I am fairly resistive to painful circumstances. For myself personally and for those with whom I share life, I would much prefer exemption from circumstances that result in physical or emotional hurt.

Of course, a lifestyle exempt from pain or other reminders of the inadequacy of our self-sufficiency only serves to provide a distorted view of our circumstances. When Moses bid farewell to the children of Israel as they were preparing to enter into the Promised Land, he cautioned them to purposefully maintain a mind-set related to their dependency upon God. He cautioned that when they were living in houses they had not built and eating from vineyards they had not planted, there would be the temptation to forget their need for God.

Moses was aware of the nature of our humanity. When our hands are full and our lives are filled with evidences of ease and comfort, we intuitively are resistive to the notion of dependency. Perhaps one of the inherent benefits of pain is the reminder of the insufficiency of our sufficiency.

Dr. Paul Brand, former medical missionary to India, states, "I now regard pain as one of the most remarkable design features of the human body and if I could choose one gift for my leprosy patients it would be the gift of pain." His conclusion was reached from personal observation, "I first learned about painlessness while working with leprosy, a disease that afflicts more than twelve million people worldwide. Leprosy has long provoked a fear bordering hysteria, mainly because of the horrible disfigurement that may result if it goes untreated. The noses of leprosy patients shrink away, their ear-lobes swell and over time they lose fingers and toes, then hands and feet. Many also go blind. Perhaps leprosy patients were destroying themselves unwittingly for the simple reason that they too lacked a system to warn them of danger."

When the ten lepers approached Christ asking for healing, one part of that request was to enable them to once again experience pain. As the one who returned to say "thank you" fell on his knees before Christ, he was probably joyously aware of the discomfort from the feel of small pebbles next to his kneecaps. In reality, the ability to experience pain serves as a subtle reminder of the limitations of our humanity. Consequently, it is only when we turn from that mind-set to God, that our needs are ultimately met.

In one of Chuck Swindoll's books, he writes, "Pain humbles the proud. It softens the stubborn. It melts the hard. Silently and relentlessly, it wins battles deep within the lonely soul. The heart alone knows its own sorrow, and not another person can fully share in it. Pain operates alone; it needs no assistance. It communicates its own message whether to statesman or servant, preacher or prodigal, mother or child. By staying, it refuses to be ignored. By hurting, it reduces its victim to profound depths of anguish. And it is at that anguishing point that the sufferer either submits and learns, developing maturity and character; or resists and becomes embittered, swamped by self-pity smothered by self will. I have tried and cannot find, either in Scripture or history, a strong willed individual whom God used greatly until he allowed him to hurt deeply."

Subsequent to earlier health problems, my life has been mostly free from circumstances that presented themselves as overwhelming or debilitating. That's not to say that there have not been periods of difficulty, high anxiety, and sadness. Through those experiences, his grace has sustained, supported, and provided calm in the midst of the storm. His grace is sufficient. His power is made perfect in weakness. It has been more than enough.

BEYOND HUMAN
INSTRUMENTALITY

SOMETIMES, POSITIVE AFFIRMATION and unexpected gifts seemingly come our way to underscore the reality of God's presence and his unconditional love. No doubt we've all had the experience of receiving a "power surge" to lift our spirits. The moments of inspiration or periods of quiet inner peace remind us that we don't live in isolation. We have a God who is loving and responsive to our needs. How refreshing it is to discover that he uses all of our life experiences to ultimately promote our greater good.

My niece was only two years old when military officials informed our family that her dad's plane had failed to return to his assigned airbase in Thailand. Although nothing detectable occurred on the radar screen, the plane had disappeared somewhere over North Vietnam. Her father was listed as "missing in action" in what later became referred to as the "Christmas bombing raids of 1972." His plane went down exactly one month to the day before the war officially ended. I, too, shared her loss. Her father was my twin brother.

Consequently, the fabric of her life has been deeply interwoven with the knowledge of what it is like living with an empty chair. It saddens her to acknowledge that most of what she remembers about her dad has been imparted through photographs and information shared with her by her mother, grandparents, and other family members.

Folks who are familiar with childhood development know that loss reexpresses itself at every developmental level. When my niece got married, unknown to any of her family members, she sewed my brother's military nametag to the inside hem of her wedding dress. She placed it on the side where her father would have been standing had he been present to give her away. Shortly before the wedding ceremony was to begin, she showed me the nametag, and we both momentarily became teary-eyed. All in all, it was a tender moment and such a thoughtful gesture on her part to honor her father in that way.

In October 2003, my niece and her husband were blessed with the birth of their first child. They named their daughter Lilian. There are not words to describe the joy and sense of ultimate fulfillment that the new role of being parents orchestrated for my niece and her husband. They were absolutely ecstatic with the responsibility and the enrichment their daughter immediately contributed to the quality of their lives.

Despite the joy, there were moments during the early months of being a new mother when my niece periodically, for a brief instant, experienced a degree of sadness over her dad's absence and the reality that her daughter will never know her grandfather. He will not be a part of her life aside from second-hand information provided by family and loved ones.

As the first Christmas approached following the birth of her daughter, my niece along with her infant daughter and another long-term friend went Christmas shopping. In one shop, my niece noticed a figurine of a man and child standing in front of the Vietnam Wall. It was in a dome container and my niece picked it up to examine it more closely. The figurine was entitled "Touch His Spirit." She looked to see if actual names were included on the two panels of "The Vietnam Wall" that were shown or if they simply looked like writing.

She had a surreal feeling when she saw the first name on the left was the name on the panel where her dad's name is listed. She followed the column down. "Ronald W. Forrester" was clearly printed on the figurine she held in her hand. She didn't have to think twice before wiping away her tears and heading for the checkout counter with this wonderful unexpected gift.

I can't even write about her experience without becoming teary-eyed, but what a wonderful sense of affirmation and reenforcement of the continued sense of family and connectedness that will always be ours.

Ultimately it was through his gift at Christmas, the birth of a savior, that makes possible the hope that is ours for eternity. My niece's unexpected discovery only serves to reenforce the eternal reality of that truth.

My character flaws are plentiful. Sadly, the way I generally manage the Christmas holidays probably falls into that category. For most of my adult years, I have been one of those people who manage to get through Christmas by purposefully easing into the experience.

I recall being asked by my wife to stop by a craft store to pick up something she needed for a project. It was mid-October. As I walked through the door, I noticed they were busily setting up their display of Christmas trees. It caught me totally off guard. I immediately did an about-face and marched out of the store. The display of artificial Christmas trees was a catalyst creating panic. My emotional response was "flight or fight," and I simply exited out the door I had entered. I just wasn't prepared to think about Christmas. I easily concluded that whatever my wife needed, she could purchase later.

A couple of weeks later, as I made my way home from work, I was blindsided again. It was as if they appeared out of nowhere. Where did these Christmas lights come from and why were they turned on? It was the first part of November. Whoever made the decision to turn on the Christmas lights was way ahead of schedule. It seemed ludicrous to me. At some level, I involuntarily chose to personalize it as an invasion of my right not to have to deal with Christmas until it was seasonally appropriate.

I mentioned my reaction to the Christmas lights to a friend who responded, "Oh, everyone is doing Christmas early this year." It was one of those "matter of fact, get on the right page" kind of statements. My friend just accepted this early rush toward Christmas as the norm. I obviously was the one who needed to alter and adjust my thinking.

"Everyone is doing Christmas early this year" has become a resounding message that has penetrated my conscious thought on a number of occasions since that time. Despite the trend, I prefer to wait until I am emotionally prepared. I prefer to wait on Christmas.

Christmas 1972 was the first time my nuclear family was not intact. My twin brother was stationed in Thailand and his squadron was regularly flying missions over Vietnam. Of course, as a family celebrating Christmas together, we verbalized thoughts related to how much we missed having my brother home for Christmas, but we were careful not to verbalize the fears and concerns that weighed most heavily on our hearts and minds.

Shortly before Christmas of that year, two of Ron's best friends were flying a mission over Vietnam and their plane was hit by a surface-to-air missile. The plane exploded on impact. Neither of the men on board escaped. My brother found the loss of his friends very upsetting. He wrote home that nothing they were doing was "worth the lives" of those two men.

Part of the problem was the continued fixed flight pattern that pilots were required to fly. Despite the fact that the Vietnamese had a fairly elaborate system of surface-to-air missiles, squadrons out of Thailand were ordered to fly the same route day after day. Military personnel planning the missions discounted the threat of the fixed surface-to-air missiles already in place. There was no variety in the route pilots were ordered to fly.

We subsequently received word that my brother's plane went down somewhere over North Vietnam two days after Christmas. His name was added to the ranks of those defined as "missing in action."

The following Christmas and many others that subsequently followed were overshadowed with the unspoken pain and sense of loss that we experienced as a family related to Ron's whereabouts. Was he a prisoner of war? Was he with the Lord? Without knowing his fate, how do you give up the hope related to a more immediate reunion than the one in the hereafter? Christmas emerged into an ongoing dread of the year for me.

As a rule of thumb, whenever I am blindsided by anything associated to Christmas, my first reaction is to panic.

The Christmas season associated to Christmas 2012 brought our nation to its knees. It was Friday, December 14, 2012. I was on a road trip to attend a work-related Christmas party about 130 miles away. It was early afternoon. I turned the radio on to listen to a regularly scheduled talk show. The voice I anticipated was not the voice that I heard. The regular afternoon broadcast had been cancelled. In its place was an ongoing report related to the tragic news coming out of Newtown, Connecticut. The report knocked the breath out of me. What tragic news! I couldn't even begin to fully comprehend the level of despair that members of that community had to be going through.

Friday's massacre of twenty-six children and adults at Sandy Hook Elementary School in Newtown elicited horror and soul-searching around the world. Until Friday, Newtown was a picturesque, affluent, picture-perfect community of twenty-seven thousand people. Today, it is a community of people who have abruptly and forcibly become painfully aware that ours is a broken world and we are broken people.

On that Friday night, hundreds of people packed St. Rose of Lima Church and stood outside in a vigil for the twenty-eight dead—twenty children and six adults at the school, the gunman's mother at home, and the gunman himself, who committed suicide. People held hands, lit candles, and sang "Silent Night."

"These twenty children were just beautiful, beautiful children," Monsignor Robert Weiss said. "These twenty children lit up this community better than all these Christmas lights we have… There are a lot brighter stars up there tonight because of these kids."

What was true of St. Rose of Lima Church reportedly was also true of other churches in the community of Newtown. Churches were filled with people collectively dealing with an overwhelming sense of sadness.

The next day found many of the townspeople of Newtown taking down their Christmas decorations. Dr. Jeannie Pasacreta, a psychologist, said, "People in my neighborhood are feeling guilty about it being Christmas. They are taking down their decorations."

According to Dan Gilgoff and Eric Marrapodi, CNN Belief Blog coeditors, "From the first moments after Friday's massacre, religious leaders were among the first people to whom worried and grieving families turned for help."

Max Lucado crafted a prayer that thoughtfully articulated our need for God in the midst of crisis and an overwhelming sense of grief.

> Dear Jesus,
>
> It's a good thing you were born at night. This world sure seems dark. I have a good eye for silver linings. But they seem dimmer lately.
>
> These killings, Lord. These children, Lord. Innocence violated. Raw evil demonstrated. The whole world seems on edge. Trigger-happy. Ticked off. We hear threats of

chemical weapons and nuclear bombs. Are we one button-push away from annihilation?

Your world seems a bit darker this Christmas. But you were born in the dark, right? You came at night. The shepherds were nightshift workers. The Wise Men followed a star. Your first cries were heard in the shadows. To see your face, Mary and Joseph needed a candle flame. It was dark. Dark with Herod's jealousy. Dark with Roman oppression. Dark with poverty. Dark with violence.

Herod went on a rampage, killing babies. Joseph took you and your mom into Egypt. You were an immigrant before you were a Nazarene.

Oh, Lord Jesus, you entered the dark world of your day. Won't you enter ours? We are weary of bloodshed. We, like the wise men, are looking for a star. We, like the shepherds, are kneeling at a manger.

This Christmas, we ask you, heal us, help us, be born anew in us.

Hopefully,
Your Children

I had driven three and a half hours to attend a Christmas stroll. The very thought of an extended Christmas party was incongruent with how I was feeling. What was true for me was also true for most of the adults at the party. News of the tragedy in Newtown had touched a chord in all of our hearts.

Newtown, Connecticut, is not the only community to experience pain and anguish orchestrated by death of children. "When Herod realized that he had been outwitted by the Magi, he was furious, and he gave orders to kill all the boys in Bethlehem and its vicinity who were two years old and under, in accordance with the time he had learned from the Magi" (Matthew 2:16).

In our Humpty Dumpty–like brokenness, we need to know that "the Lord is close to the brokenhearted and saves those who are crushed in spirit" (Psalms 34:18).

In contrast, the Christmas season of 2010 will be forever recorded in my memory as though it were etched in stone. I will remember it for as long as I live. I had been in Houston for several days and was driving home to Austin. It was late in the evening of December 3, 2010. When I turned on the radio, I was startled by the sound of Christmas music filling my car. Intuitively, I quickly hit the seek button to advance to another radio station. I was greeted with more Christmas music. Again, I hit the seek button and found another station playing a Christmas song. Protectively, I chose to turn the radio off. I just wasn't prepared to think about Christmas.

I was content to drive in silence, lost in thought. At some point in my commute, out of nowhere, the tune and the lyrics to "I'll Be Home for Christmas" began to roll around in my head. Surprisingly I didn't attempt to redirect my thoughts. It was a pleasant experience. I couldn't remember if it was Perry Como or Frank Sinatra who sang the song. For some strange reason, I delighted in the sound. It didn't even have a religious connotation, but I was very content to let the song roll around in my head.

Uncharacteristically, the experience was very comfortable for me. It was similar to sharing a cup of hot flavored coffee with a treasured friend or sitting in a comfortable chair reading a book. It felt like home. It was warm and comforting.

Who would have thought the next day I'd receive a telephone call from my brother telling me that my mother's health circumstances were rapidly deteriorating and that death was imminent? My wife and I caught the next flight, and before day's end, I was standing at her bedside.

As I stood in mother's room at the nursing home attempting to process everything I was seeing and what I'd just been told about her condition, a thousand thoughts filled my head. Interestingly, all those were subsequently replaced with the duplication of my experience from the day before. The tune and lyrics to "I'll Be

Home for Christmas" gave me the assurance that everything was going to be all right. It almost put a smile on my face.

Because of God's gift of Christmas, the promises of Christ ring true, "Peace I leave with you; My peace I give you. I do not give to you as the world gives. Do not let your hearts be troubled and do not be afraid" (John 14:27).

Knowing that mother was home for Christmas was such a source of peace for me. It really was an answer to prayer. For the past three and a half years before her death, I'd prayed for my mother on a regular basis. I'd asked God for her healing.

In asking, I didn't know if God would choose to restore her cognitive abilities or if he would ultimately heal the brokenness of her humanity. Just as one day, a caterpillar pauses to allow nature to form a cocoon only to emerge weeks later a beautiful butterfly, so it is with death. God heals the brokenness of our humanity in order that we might live forever.

Mother's illness took from her the cognitive ability to live relationally or even to exercise independence in having her basic needs met. It was very unsettling for all of us to see her in that condition.

Over the preceding three and a half years before her home-coming, I never reached the point of thinking my prayers were unheard, but I often wondered what God wanted to teach us through this. The scripture says, "All things work together for good to them that love God to them who are the called according to his purpose" (Romans 8:28).

The lessons to be learned weren't for Mother. She had already mastered the lessons for life. They were for us.

- Was it simply for us to be content in whatever circumstances came our way? Throughout Mother's illness, she never seemed unhappy or discontent. Was it a message that we, too, needed to be content?

- Was it the need for us to learn to live with a higher dependency on him?

- Was it a reminder that faith is a journey—the assurance of things hoped for, the evidence of things not seen (Hebrews 11:1)?

As long as I have the wonderful gift of memory, I can return again and again to the treasured recollection of days gone by. I can remember with gratitude the love and influence that helped me navigate my formative years and continue to provide strength and resourcefulness as I meet the needs of this day. It really is more than enough.

THE MEASURE OF A MAN

Two or three hours before my dad died, the registered nurse at the hospital who was responsible for his care stopped me in the hallway outside his room and asked, "Who is William Forrester?" Initially, I thought I'd heard her incorrectly. (Hearing or lack of hearing is one of the things I inherited from my dad.) It was about 3:30 a.m., and I wasn't fully alert. "I beg your pardon" is the only coherent response I could make.

"Who is William Forrester?" she repeated. "Isn't he a famous writer? They were saying in the nurse's station that William Forrester is an award-winning author." I simply smiled at the twenty-something-year-old standing in front of me and said, "You've got the wrong Forrester in mind. My dad doesn't write books." (Apparently someone in the nurse's station had seen the movie *Finding Forrester* that chronicles the life and activities of a reclusive writer named William Forrester.)

Later that morning, following my father's death, as I was attempting to drift off to sleep, I thought again about the young nurse's question "Who is William Forrester?" The question still sounded strange. William is my dad's first name. His middle name, the name he answered to, is Wayne. Yet it was a question worth contemplating. Who is William Forrester? This time, a thousand and one thoughts filled my mind as I contemplated possible responses to her question:

- Who is William Forrester?

My dad wasn't famous. He lived simply, and yet at the same time, he lived purposefully. Although he wasn't famous, that's not to say he was unimportant. To those of us who called him "dad," "papaw," "uncle," "brother," "cousin," "friend"…we don't have the words to express his range of influence or the impact his love and care had in our lives. We will forever be enriched by the gift of having shared life with him.

My first year in college, I received a letter from my dad. That in and of itself was a surprise because to my knowledge my dad didn't write letters. That was a detail delegated for my mother to handle. The letter was one of affirmation and support, acknowledging how proud Dad was of me and how grateful he was that I was his son. It left me speechless.

Ten to fifteen years later, I sent Dad a similar letter, acknowledging how grateful and proud I was of him for being a wonderful grandfather to my children. I couldn't have selected anyone better. The transformation astonished me.

It was clear to me thirty years ago that Dad was obviously not the same man I grew up with. He was patient, attentive, incredibly kind, always available. He always went the second and third mile to ensure his grandchildren knew how special they were and how much they were loved.

What I now know from the vantage point of "mature adulthood" is that my dad didn't change; he was always the same. Perhaps children have to reach mature adulthood before they develop the cognitive skill of really getting to know their parents. How grateful I am that my dad and I shared a friendship in the midst of adulthood.

• Who is William Forrester?

My dad's life was defined in part by the environment in which he grew up.

Dad was raised as one of two children on a family farm in Montague County. He "came of age" during the Great Depression and the imprint from that experience forever colored his perception of the potential for the "worst possible case scenario."

Dad's family never went hungry; they either planted and grew what they needed, or they bartered for what they were without. However, it was clearly a contrast to the decade of affluence in which most of my generation can relate and one in which my dad was never completely comfortable.

One of the dreaded questions Dad often asked during my adolescent years when I wanted something was "How much does it cost?" Dad knew the value of hard work, and he knew the value of a dime. Throughout his life, given the choice, Dad would prefer to have the dime rather than what it would buy.

Over the last six months of his life, Dad was repeatedly in and out of the hospital. With every hospital readmission, the first major hurdle was to help Dad accept the fact that his physical well-being and comfort were far more important than his financial portfolio.

Dad calculated to the penny what each hospital admission cost. Perhaps he had already figured out he didn't always get his money's worth. A couple of weeks before his death, he told me, with some degree of frustration, that he had hoped to have something left over after he was gone to leave to us. He wasn't sure at his current rate of spending that he was going to be able to accomplish that goal. That saddened him.

My dad was part of that generation who saved the world. Tom Brokaw defined it in his book as the "Greatest Generation"—that WWII generation where values, duty, honor, economy, courage, service, love of family and country, and above all, responsibility for oneself, defined one's approach to life. That all set the precedent for who Dad was and the values and courage he represented.

• Who is William Forrester?

In a lot of ways, I wish I were more like my dad. He always colored between the lines… He was a no-nonsense, play it by the book, "do what you're supposed to do" kind of guy. In other words, Dad has always been responsible.

During Dad's repeated hospital stays, when his physical stamina wasn't as steadfast as it needed to be to support his independence, I never worried about him doing anything foolish that might result in his harm.

I told each of the admitting nurses, "If you don't want him getting out of bed or attempting to walk without assistance, all you have to do is tell him. Because my dad always does what he's supposed to do."

I can't count on one hand the number of times I'd push dad in the wheelchair outside the rehab facility to enjoy the outdoors. Every time he would remind me, "Don't get me in the sun. I'm not supposed to be in the sun." Dad followed instructions to the letter.

One of the nurses in the intensive care unit saw that Dad was having a lot of difficulty breathing. He told him to take deep slow breaths and don't talk. Just relax and breathe. Don't talk. About ten seconds later, the doctor came in and started asking Dad a number of questions. When she was gone, he looked at me, shook his head, and said, "I wish they'd get their story straight. One person tells me don't talk. The next person comes in and starts asking questions. How am I supposed to know what to do?"

Dad always colored between the lines. At least I think he did. There is only one recent situation that might be questionable. I'll probably regret sharing this, but my dad had an addiction. It is obviously a dominant gene because I share it as well. It is an addiction to Mentholatum.

The use of Mentholatum for one's lips and nose has been a daily ritual in our family dating back to as long as I can remember. One of the respiratory therapists at the rehab center noticed the Mentholatum jar on Dad's bedside table. In a stern authoritarian voice she said, "Mr. Forrester, Mentholatum is a petroleum product. You are on oxygen. You are not supposed to use that. If there was a spark it could ignite."

Dad simply looked at her and meekly said, "Okay."

After the therapist was gone, I moved the jar, but I ensured Dad knew where I put it. As I was leaving, I told him that if it were me, I'd take the chance. He simply smiled.

Dad did tell me toward the end of his life that if he had his life to live over, he would have done some of it differently. He said, "After the war, I did some things I'm not proud of. God has forgiven me, but I still wish I had done it differently."

I responded, "Dad, I've never been in a war, but I, too, have done some things I'm not proud of. I, too, wish I had done it differently. I guess that makes us both more appreciative of God's unconditional love and the whole concept of grace."

"You're right."

• Who is William Forrester?

I read somewhere years ago that the best gift a father can give his children is the gift of loving their mother. The relationship Dad and Mother shared as husband and wife was one worth noting. They were married sixty-one years. Theirs was a relationship of love. It was a relationship of mutual respect, admiration, and support.

For the last eight years of my dad's life, the passion and the motivation that kept him going was the simple desire to provide for my mother's needs. After her illness leveled her ability to maintain their home, prepare meals, or even take care of herself, Dad stepped up to the plate and lovingly and caringly provided for every detail.

I honestly don't know how he did it, particularly over the last fourteen months of his life when he himself needed a primary caretaker because of his illness. He denied that fact in order to provide for Mom.

Until his dying breath, Dad's primary concern was to ensure Mother was going to be cared for and that her needs would be met. Even the week before his death, he articulated again his desire to get well so he could bring her home. With tears streaming down his cheeks, he said, "I really miss her."

In one of Max Lucado's books he asks the question,

> Are a bride and groom ever more married than they are the first day? The vows are made and the certificate signed—could they be any more married than that?
>
> Perhaps they could. Imagine them fifty years later. Four kids later. A trio of transfers and a cluster of valleys and victories later. After half a century of marriage, they finish each other's sentences and order each other's food. They even start looking alike after a while. Wouldn't they have to be more married on their fiftieth anniversary than on their wedding day?
>
> Yet, on the other hand, how could they be? The marriage certificate hasn't matured. Ah, but the relationship has, and there is the difference. Technically, they are no more united than they were when they left the altar. But relationally they are completely different. Marriage is both a done deal and a daily development, something you did and something you do.

What a legacy is mine. Dad didn't just talk about love. He demonstrated it. "Greater love hath no one than this: to lay down one's life for one's friend" (John 15:13).

•   Who is William Forrester?

The last year of Dad's life was marked by one physical difficulty after another. Yet despite problem after problem, he refused to give up or to retreat to bitterness or to fall prey to lasting depression. He knew that God would take care of the tomorrows, and he was intent on living the todays.

Dad's approach to the problem of broken health was very much like the psalmist who said, "Yeah, though I walk through the valley of the shadow of death, I will fear no evil for thou art with me, thy rod and thy staff they comfort me" (Psalm 23:4).

Dad told me on a number of occasions not to worry. He was going to be fine either way this turned out. He'd either recover or he'd be with Jesus. Either way, it was going to be okay. He was going home.

There is so much about Dad's life that I valued. Even seven years later, I think of him often with a sense of gratitude. He continues to be present with me through his influence, his values, and through the knowledge that very much like the potter, he shaped my life. That is more than enough.

" WHERE IS GOD WHEN IT HURTS ? "

THE SCARS ON both shins finally faded. After two and a half months, I was beginning to think they would perpetually serve as a visual reminder of things that "go bump in the dark."

It was nighttime when we arrived at my brother-in-law's house. We've always considered ourselves "back door" company so we drove around to the back of the house to more easily access entrance to the house from the back door. The carport was dark, but light coming from the interior of the house cast enough light to guide our path.

When we started walking, I noticed a tractor parked in the carport and remember thinking it a strange place to store equipment. Most people would opt for car storage rather than farm equipment. At least, from my way of thinking, it was simply another illustration that my brother-in-law doesn't always adapt to conventional thinking.

Following our visit, we headed back toward our car. I noticed the tractor again, but with the light behind us, I didn't notice the tractor blade. It has been said that I only walk at one speed—fast. When I circumvented the tractor, I had no idea that in short order I'd be sprawled facedown on the drive with incredible pain coming from both legs.

I don't know who was more surprised, my wife or me. She quickly made a need's assessment, asked if anything was broken and expressed her intent to summon help from inside the house. I was still facedown on the driveway attempting to summon the strength to get off the ground. "No, no, no…I'm fine. Don't go for help! I'm okay, just give me a minute!" Panic almost set in. The last thing I wanted was to have an audience watching me get off the ground and no doubt subsequently limp toward the car.

"Ouch, ouch, ouch" continued to resonate in my head. How incredibly careless of me to fall over a tractor blade! It was little wonder that I didn't actually do some real damage.

With the exception of a three-to-six inch gash on both legs where the skin was scraped off, I was good to go, but the residual pain served as a reminder that I should pay closer attention to details.

In reflecting back on that experience, I am quickly reminded of how often things can go awry. Other than a brief bout with a little discomfort, no real damage was done. But every time I pass a fender-bender at a roadway intersection, or hear a siren, or see an ambulance, I am reminded that someone's life has abruptly changed. Perhaps they may not have the good fortune of bouncing back as easily.

For some, a ringing telephone in the middle of the night, a knock at the door, a follow-up at the doctor's office to review the outcome of medical tests, all carry with them the potential for life to abruptly change.

James wrote, "Why, you do not even know what will happen tomorrow. What is your life? You are a mist that appears for a little while and then vanishes" (James 4:14). Each of us must live with the notion that the status quo of the hour doesn't necessarily ensure any guarantee for the future.

About a year ago I was in Oklahoma City for a meeting. While I was there, I purposefully went to tour the Oklahoma City National Memorial honoring the victims, survivors, and rescuers from the bombing of the Murrah Federal Building on April 19, 1995. Actually, I made two visits to the site. I saw it first during the night and subsequently in the daytime. Both venues defy description. It is an impressive and awe-inspiring tribute.

The memorial includes two large walls or twin gates framing the moment of destruction. The east gate is marked 9:01 a.m. on April 19. That east gate represents the innocence of the city. The west gate is marked 9:03 a.m. on April 19. It represents the moment Oklahoma City was forever changed. It also is a testimony of the hope that subsequently replaced the horror in the moments and days following the bombing.

There is a very large reflection pool with gently flowing water. It is subtle, but the calming sound of the flowing water orchestrates a peaceful setting for quiet thoughts. The reflection pool is impressive, but it was the field of empty chairs crafted in bronze that brought tears to my eyes. One hundred sixty-eight chairs were located in nine rows. There was one row for each floor of the building. Each chair was engraved with the name of someone killed on that floor. Nineteen smaller chairs represented the children who were killed in the explosion.

There is something about the serenity of the setting that makes talking seem inappropriate or disrespectful. It fully captures both sadness and hope. I can only imagine the range of emotions that someone who experienced loss up-close and personal on April 19, 1995, as a result of the calculated destruction that leveled the Murrah Federal Building would experience in visiting the monument.

Have you ever asked yourself the question, "Where is God when it hurts?" Periodically across the years, I have revisited the question time and time again in the thought processes of my mind. As one year ended and the next began, I found myself lost in the same kind of contemplative questioning and thoughtfulness. I looked beyond my own issues and concerns to the challenges and obstacles faced by several people I knew. I attempted to look at life from their vantage point. As their pastor, friend, or extended family member, I couldn't ignore their plight. Whether directly or indirectly, they were all asking the same kind of questions: "Could their faith in God make a tangible difference in the context of their life experiences?"

It is my belief that whatever life brought their way, what they believed about God and his involvement in their lives would ultimately color their perception of life. They would either negotiate life from the vantage point of hopefulness or hopelessness depending on their perception of God. After all, do we see God as an absentee landlord or is he intimately involved in our lives through a loving relationship established through Christ? Is it not true that what we believe about God, his love, his involvement, his abiding presence, and his ongoing strength will alter our perception of what the New Year brings?

In order to test my premise, I jotted down the following notes the first week of the New Year:

- One Wednesday of this past week, a mother asked me to pray for her son. Her son confided to her by telephone on Christmas day that he was having a difficult time. He said he felt as though he didn't "fit in" anywhere. He felt lonely and alienated. He was out of work and down on his luck. He only had one question: "Why doesn't anything ever work out for me?" It was a tough question. In attempting to offer words of encouragement, I suggested to the mother that she might remind her son that tough times don't last forever. She looked at me and responded, "My son is only thirty-one, but most of his life has been a tough time. I am very concerned."

- A couple in their mid-seventies began the New Year facing life-threatening medical issues. The husband who already had a myriad of health concerns began treatment for throat cancer on January 2. I talked to his wife at the end of December and expressed my concern and sadness related to their circumstances. Her response was somewhat stoic: "We don't have a choice." As I hung up the telephone, I couldn't help wonder what the New Year would hold for them.

- I thought about a friend who opted for early retirement because he didn't like the new role prescribed him by his company. Consequently, he began his own company. The change obviously represents opportunity, but it also represents loss. Long-term working relationships have ended, and he no longer has the same circle of support. What does the New Year hold for him?

From the vantage point of a year later, the young man who was struggling at the beginning of the year was still struggling at the beginning of the following year. His primary question continues to be the same: "Why doesn't anything ever work out for me?"

The man with throat cancer died on Christmas day. The last year of his life was filled with overwhelming health-related issues and difficulty. Yet in the midst of life's greatest challenges, the family found the faith and strength to trust God in the midst of their sadness. At his funeral, one of the family members read the poem "My First Christmas in Heaven." I had not heard it before and found its expression of faith sustaining and supportive.

Christmas in Heaven

I see the countless Christmas trees around the world below
With tiny lights, like heaven's stars, reflecting in the snow.
The sight is so spectacular, please wipe away the tear
For I am spending Christmas with Jesus Christ this year.

I hear the many Christmas songs that people hold so dear
But the sounds of music can't compare
with the Christmas choir up here.

I have no words to tell you, the joy their voices bring,
For it is beyond description, to hear the angels sing.

I know how much you miss me,
I see the pain inside your heart,
But I am not so far away,
We really aren't apart.

So be happy for me, dear ones,
You know I hold you dear,
And be glad I'm spending Christmas
with Jesus Christ this year.

I sent you each a special gift,
From my heavenly home above,
I sent you each a memory of my undying love.

After all, love is a gift more precious than pure gold,
It was always most important in the stories Jesus told.

Please love and keep each other,
As my father said to do,
For I can't count the blessings or love
he has for each of you.

So have a Merry Christmas and wipe away the tear,
Remember, I am spending Christmas
with Jesus Christ this year.

The friend who opted for early retirement and started his
own company couldn't be happier. Despite the losses of the past,
he has discovered that God is still God and capable of pouring

meaning and purpose into life. His faith walk has been a spring-board for positive change.

Cynthia Clawson, the most talented and compassionate Christian vocalist that I have ever met, has a heart for children and families who come from hard places. On one of her albums, she recorded a song that begs the question, "Where is God when it hurts?" The song is entitled "Georgia Lee."

> Cold was the night, hard was the ground
> They found her in a small grove of trees
> Lonesome was the place where Georgia was found
> She's too young to be out on the street.
>
> Why wasn't God watching?
> Why wasn't God listening?
> Why wasn't God there for Georgia Lee?
>
> Ida said she couldn't keep Georgia
> From dropping out of school
> I was doing the best that I could
> But she kept runnin' away from this world
> These children are so hard to raise good
>
> Why wasn't God watching?
> Why wasn't God listening?
> Why wasn't God there for Georgia Lee?
>
> Close your eyes and count to ten
> I will go and hide but then
> Be sure to find me, I want you to find me
> And we'll play all over
> We'll play all over
> We'll play all over again
>
> There's a toad in the witch grass
> There's a crow in the corn
> Wild flowers on a cross by the road

And somewhere a baby is crying for her mom
As the hills turn from green back to gold

Why wasn't God watching?
Why wasn't God listening?
Why wasn't God there for Georgia Lee?

Why wasn't God watching?
Why wasn't God listening?
Why wasn't God there for Georgia Lee?

It was on a Saturday morning, a couple of days after the mas-sacre and carnage that left twelve dead and thirty-one injured at Ft. Hood on November 5, 2009. I left home at the crack of dawn to take my pickup into town to get the windshield replaced. Because I got there very early, I was the first customer of the day at the glass company. Rather than allowing me to sit in a corner of the showroom, I was ushered into the employee break room where the television was turned on and a news reporter was recapping the news associated with the aftermath of the tragedy at Ft. Hood.

In addition, two employees were finishing their breakfast, and the day's newspaper was neatly folded on a table. There was also the promise of fresh coffee as soon as it finished brewing.

Despite the kindness of the employee who directed me to the enclosed break-room, my first thought was I liked it better in the showroom. For one thing, there was more light in the showroom. In addition, it felt a little awkward watching folks have break-fast. I didn't even realize I was hungry until I saw their plates. It also felt like I was eavesdropping on their conversation. That was clearly not my intent.

It was awkward. I picked up the newspaper and was immedi-ately inundated with news and information related to the terrible tragedy surrounding Ft. Hood. The mere thought of the level of grief and despair that so many families were experiencing was very saddening. Of course, the news broadcast was generating the same information including pictures and information on those whose lives had been taken. It was almost information overload.

Several of the soldiers interviewed on Saturday morning referenced their acknowledgment of their need for help in dealing with the aftermath of Thursday's massacre. At the same time, they expressed confusion in knowing where to find help. After all, the person responsible for the horrific nightmare in which they found themselves was a major in the US Army and a psychiatrist, representing the highest credentials of those in the mental health field. If he couldn't be trusted, who can you trust?

I diverted my attention from the television and became absorbed in the newspaper. Yet out of my peripheral hearing, I vaguely heard the television reporter mentioning a young preacher in Virginia, an alumni of Virginia Tech, who had written a "soon to be released" book regarding the massacre at Virginia Tech on April 16, 2007, that took the lives of thirty people. The tile of the book was *Should We Fire God: Dealing With A God Who Doesn't Seem To Be Doing His Job*.

That caught my attention. I found myself fumbling to find a pen and something to write on. I wanted to at least remember the author's name. Reportedly, Jim Pace, author and Virginia Tech alumni, explains why God sometimes allows life to go terribly wrong and how to maintain faith in spite of calamity.

I subsequently discovered on a Google search that the book was released in April 2010. In addition, a friend and colleague of Jim Pace, Matt Rogers had also written about the same experience. He entitled his book *When Answers Aren't Enough: Experiencing God as Good When Life Isn't*.

Matt Rogers wrote, "I'm a pastor. I know how to reconcile a good God with an often evil world. I could give those answers in my sleep. But what should I do when those simple solutions fail to satisfy? When the sadness is heavy and sinking and answers are not enough? I believe God is good. But how do I experience

Him as good when grief is raining down? After the massacre at Virginia Tech on April 16, 2007, this seemed as relevant as any topic I could tackle. I wrote the book for myself, for my fellow Hokies, and for anyone stuck in grief. Sooner or later, we all will be."

Over forty years ago, when I was an idealistic, young college student, I worked as an orderly in the emergency room of a large hospital. The experience proved to be one of the most educational venues of my life. In three short years, I witnessed enough trauma to last a lifetime. Some of those memories continue to be as clear as if they happened yesterday.

It was around 2:00 a.m. A car pulled into the portico that served as an entrance reserved for use by ambulance drivers. I was working the 11:00 p.m. to 7:00 a.m. shift that night. When no one immediately came inside, I walked outside to ask if I could be of assistance.

Family members in the car almost reverently passed out to me a four-year-old child whose body appeared lifeless. I carried her immediately to one of the treatment rooms and summoned the nurse and doctor. Sadly, there was nothing they could do.

Earlier in the evening the family had rushed both children to another hospital after discovering the two sisters had eaten rat poison. The poison was located under the kitchen sink in their grandmother's home. The mother and her two daughters were visiting from California. The hospital that initially treated the children had given them a liquid medication to cause them to expel the contents of their stomachs. That reportedly was the extent of the medical treatment provided. They were then released to go back to their grandparent's home.

The grandfather asked to use the telephone and summoned his pastor to come to the emergency waiting room. I overheard the pastor as he provided counsel to this grieving mother and her family. He said simply, "We don't understand this, but we have to accept it as God's will."

"We don't understand this, but we have to accept it as God's will," seemingly was the mantra and extent of the pastoral counseling I observed and overheard during my three years of employment at the hospital.

It all seemed so incongruent with my perception of God. It didn't take long or many exposures to awful circumstances for me to begin wondering what kind of God do we serve if this really is his will?

God is with us and he cares. God is with us, and because of his presence, he can make all things new.

Horatio G. Spafford penned the words to the hymn "It Is Well with My Soul" following two major traumas in his life. The Chicago fire of October 1871 ruined him financially. A short time later, all four of his daughters died when the ship they were on collided with another ship. His wife, who was traveling with their daughters, survived. She later sent her husband a telegram which stated simply, "Saved alone."

Several weeks later, as Horatio Spafford traveled abroad, at approximately the same place where his daughters perished at sea, the Holy Spirit inspired him to write the words of this well-known hymn. They beautifully addressed his ability to face the future with hope and confidence in the sufficiency of God's sustaining grace.

I have the good fortune of sharing a friendship with someone of Horatio Spafford's character. Never have I known anyone who represents such unfaltering faith or confidence in the sustaining sufficiency of God's grace. My life has been greatly enriched from observing his "trust walk."

When we first met, Eric Groten, my friend, was negotiating the painful circumstance of divorce and the agonies associated with sharing custody of one's children. Just prior to our meeting, he also had been abruptly thrust in the precipitously painful process of managing the sense of loss and grief resulting from the untimely deaths of his twin brother and his niece and two nephews. Their lives had been forfeited by the careless and uncon-scionable actions of an intoxicated truck driver.

Through it all, God provided the resources he needed. The prophet Isaiah describes it as the ability "to walk and not become weary" (Isaiah 40:31). I saw it demonstrated in my friend's life.

Approximately a year later, Eric's two children were killed along with their mother in a plane crash. Again, somehow he managed to "walk and not become weary." He credits the success and periodic struggles and pitfalls of that painful journey to the proven dependability of God's love. He intuitively and percepti-bly knows that God's healing will always be a work in progress.

A subsequent telephone call from Eric several months later notifying me of the birth of his son left me with tears streaming down my face. Without doubt it was through divine providence, but his son's birth date marked the first anniversary of his chil-dren's deaths. Even now as I write them, the memory of his words leave me teary-eyed: "We are feeling very well indeed—mind, body and soul."

As I subsequently reflected on the wonderful news shared by Eric, I am reminded of the promise that God made to Job. Despite the difficulties and losses that Job had experienced, God reminded him that he was still God. He could be relied on to provide for the needs of tomorrow.

Eric's life is a miracle. He has confronted issues and circum-stances that would immobilize others. I have heard it said that people emerge from tragedy with one of two outcomes. They either become better or they become bitter. Perhaps the key to my friend's success and his humble spirit is his acknowledgement that somehow God has provided.

Fortunately, life is not ultimately defined by "things that go bump in the dark." His resurrection proves that light is eternally triumphant over darkness and life is eternally victorious over death. That which matters most is the gift of Easter. Because of that, life shared with the awareness of Christ is more than enough.

LIFE'S INSTRUCTION BOOK

HAVE YOU EVER wondered, "Why didn't I write that?" A couple of books that made the *New York Times* best seller list come to mind. *Life's Little Instruction Book* was written as a father's gift to his son when the son left for college. It was simply a reminder of some common sense kinds of things to remember. Simple stuff:

- Don't forget to polish your shoes.
- Never go to bed with dirty dishes in the sink.
- Look people in the eye and have a firm handshake.
- Leave everything better than you found it.
- Call your mother.

The list of helpful and practical suggestions is irrefutable. They make perfect sense. It is not rocket science. It is the kind of ongoing information most of us were provided in the course of our childhood. Jackson Brown had the presence of mind to write it all down and provide it to his son as a primer for life. It subsequently was a *New York Times* best seller for fifty weeks. What an incredibly well-written book.

The Book of Questions is another thought-provoking book that at face value doesn't seem that difficult. It is simply a book of questions, but those questions are thought-provoking and often serve as the basis for conversation starters or for getting to know others at something other than a surface level. It, too, was on the *New York Times* best seller list.

Some of the questions are not easily answered:

- If you were to die this evening with no opportunity to communicate with anyone, what would you most regret not having told someone? Why haven't you told them?

- You discover your wonderful one-year-old child is, because of a mix-up at the hospital, not yours. Would you want to exchange the child to try to correct the mistake?

- When was the last time you stole anything? Would you return it now if you could?

Not so well known is a list of *Things I've Learned* by Jack Longley, previous pastor of Trinity Presbyterian Church in San Jose, California. He writes:

- I've learned that you cannot make someone love you. All you can do is be someone who can be loved. The rest is up to them.

- I've learned that no matter how much I care, some people just don't care back.

- I've learned that it takes years to build up trust, and only seconds to destroy it.

- I've learned that it's not what you have in your life but who you have in your life that counts.

- I've learned that you can get by on charm for about fifteen minutes; after that, you'd better know something!

- I've learned that you can do something in an instant that will give you heartache for life.

- I've learned that you can keep going long after you can't!

- I've learned that we are responsible for what we do, no matter how we feel!

- I've learned that either you control your attitude or it controls you.

- I've learned that heroes are the people who do what has to be done when it needs to be done, regardless of the consequences.

- I've learned that money is a lousy way of keeping score.

- I've learned that sometimes when I'm angry I have the right to be angry, but that doesn't give me the right to be cruel.

- I've learned that maturity has more to do with what types of experiences you've had and what you've learned from them and less to do with how many birthdays you've celebrated.

- I've learned that no matter how good a friend is, they're going to hurt you every once in a while and you must forgive them for that.

- I've learned that it isn't always enough to be forgiven by others. Sometimes you are to learn to forgive yourself.

- I've learned that our background and circumstances may have influenced who we are, but we are responsible for who we become!

- I've learned that we don't have to change friends if we understand that friends change.

- I've learned that no matter how you try to protect your children, they will eventually get hurt and you will hurt in the process.

- I've learned that your life can be changed in a matter of hours by people who don't even know you.

- I've learned that even when you think you have no more to give, when a friend cries out to you, you will find the strength to help.

- I've learned that it's hard to determine where to draw the line between being nice and not hurting people's feelings, and standing up for what you believe.

- I've learned that the people you care about most in life are taken from you too soon!

There is little I can add to Rev. Longley's list, but let me suggest six or seven other variables or life lessons that need to be added to life's instruction book.

Lesson one: Periodically choose to operate outside your comfort zone and be open to experiencing new things.

It has been twelve years, but I remember it well. I was obligated. There was simply no way out. The previous weekend, my wife had accompanied me to an engagement party for a family member of my employer. It was now my turn to be conciliatory. I don't know who came up with the slogan "Turnabout is fair play," but after being married the vast majority of my life, I knew my wife's thought processes well enough to know the die was cast.

I was now obligated to accompany her to the seventieth birthday party for one of the senior partners in the law firm where she is employed. I won't say that I went kicking and screaming; I have a little more finesse than that, but I approached the evening as though I was scheduled for a root canal at the dentist's office. It was something I clearly did not want to do.

When it comes to large groups of people I don't know, my natural tendency is that of an introvert. Most of the people I know would refute that because I've spent years overcompensating. They would probably describe me more as a party animal than a wallflower, but that is only because I generally have some control over the groups I find myself in the midst of and the size of the group. As a rule of thumb, I avoid groups where I don't know anyone. After all, my absence would be undetected because they don't know me either.

In this case, I went, knowing that the group would represent about three hundred of the honoree's closest friends and associates plus one straggler who was there only out of a sense of obligation to his wife.

Much to my surprise, the evening proved to be absolutely contrary to my preconceived expectations. The first person I was introduced to was one of the sons of the honoree who graciously thanked us for coming. Next I met the honoree who was even more pronounced in his acknowledgement that he was pleased we were there. In the space of a few minutes, my wife introduced me to at least fifteen people who seemed very much at ease and were friendly and hospitable. My fears associated with being thrust in the midst of a group of three hundred strangers dissipated immediately.

The highlight of the evening was twofold. Family members and colleagues of the honoree shared personal reflections. The honoree then had an opportunity to provide his insight related to some of the stories shared.

From the first words spoken, it became clear that the honoree was well-respected, honored, and genuinely loved by those who participated. Those who spoke did so, not out of a sense of obligation but out of a personal desire to articulate words of gratitude and thanksgiving for the range of influence and importance the honoree held in their lives. The emotion shared was something that could not be fabricated. All those who spoke shared a debt of gratitude that was genuine and forthright.

The thing that most amazed me was the honoree himself. He is without doubt one of the most skilled orators to be found anywhere. His presentation was articulate, thoughtful, and very entertaining. He clearly has the ability to think on his feet and has a captivating presence. He breaks all of the stereotypes associated with being seventy years of age.

I emerged from the evening with a sense of gratitude that my wife had challenged my comfort level and had insisted that I accompany her to what proved to be a delightful evening. Left to my own devices, I would have missed a very enjoyable evening and would have forfeited the opportunity to meet some really nice and talented people.

I may be stretching the scripture where Jesus said, "Judge not lest you be judged" (Matthew 7:1), but I wonder how many of us miss opportunities to enhance our lives because we judgmentally refuse to move beyond our comfort zones. We purposefully and judgmentally choose to avoid people, circumstances, and opportunities because we are not open to moving beyond the status quo and stretching our boundaries. We may be missing the icing on the cake, which is, incidentally, the best part.

I also emerged from the evening with this thought. For years I have said tongue-in-cheek, if my wife had killed me the first time she thought about it, she'd be out of prison by now. After meeting Roy Minton, I'm convinced she'd never serve time. He has the skill level and expertise to ensure she would never spend a night in jail.

Lesson two: If you keep doing what you've always done, you'll keep getting the same results you've always gotten. If you desire a different outcome, you have to do it differently.

A little over two years ago, I was looking through a filing cabinet at home and came across a written report related to an MRI of my lower back. The report was dated January 2002. Seeing the date was somewhat of a shock for me. Had I really been dealing with back and leg pain for ten years?

As I stood in the garage where the filing cabinet is located, holding the report in my hand, I remembered that one doctor, a neurologist who initially provided consultation, told me that the only way to correct the problem was surgically. He counseled that

I should do the surgery then while I was still relatively young and healthy. He was not a surgeon, but he was willing to make a referral. At about the same time, my primary care physician told me, "No, don't have surgery until you have explored every other alternative and have no other option." His caution was stern, "There are no guarantees that come with back surgery."

Truthfully, even if my primary care physician hadn't suggested that I try other options, I am sure I would have taken every other possible alternative before I seriously considered surgery. The long and short of it, I avoid pain whenever possible. They can call the surgery minimally invasive if they want to, but recovery is always a painful process.

Consequently, I did everything imaginable to resolve the issue without surgery. I started with physical therapy. It was inconvenient, but I went twice a week and actually followed through with the physical exercises they suggested. It didn't make an appreciable difference.

My primary care physician subsequently referred me to pain management specialists. I can't recall how many different physicians or how many different prescriptions I was provided over the course of ten years, but at the end of the day, it didn't make a difference.

From there, I graduated to back injections. Fortunately, I was under anesthesia when those were administered. Did they help? They may have helped temporarily, but the pain relief was short-lived.

How about nontraditional methods? Never say I'm not flexible. I colored way outside the lines looking for helpful alternatives. Next to my fear of snakes, fear of needles comes closest to promoting a panic attack for me. For a period of time, I actually went for acupuncture. I was surprised to discover the needles didn't hurt. I actually told the acupuncturist that if he learned I had been to the reptile house at the zoo, to please refer me for a mental health assessment. My fear of needles was closely akin to my fear of snakes. Since I was no longer afraid of needles, I didn't want to get too carried away.

I can't truthfully tell you that I found the acupuncture helpful, but I gave it the ole college try. When the acupuncturist suggested I start drinking a special formula of herbs in addition to the acupuncture treatments, I was even open to that for a limited period of time. It took about an hour and a half every other day to brew the herbs. The smell was anything but pleasing. I don't have the words to accurately describe the taste. Actually I do, but I prefer not to talk like that. Let me simply say, it was not palatable. After a couple of months with no tangible improvement or reduction of leg and back pain, I opted to go back to more traditional methods.

Standing in the garage, written MRI report in hand, I resolved I didn't have another ten years to waste. If surgery was an alternative that could help, I wanted it now, not ten years from now. I had already wasted enough time. Consequently, I made an appointment with a surgeon the following week.

A year later, I'm guardedly optimistic that I've handled the back and leg pain issue. I can check that one off my list. I've told any number of people that I still have lots of steps in front of me. There are many places I want to go and many things I want to see, and I want to experience it all as pain free as possible.

A six-week recovery process is a wonderful trade out for a future of pain-free living. The discomfort I experienced actually wasn't as difficult as I anticipated. I knew going in that post-operatively there would be pain associated with the process. You can't have one without having the other. Going for six weeks without lifting anything over five pounds was the most difficult challenge. That pretty well limits you to not picking up anything that weighs more than a dinner plate.

On a very different dimension, as important as my back is, my physical body including the back only serves its purpose this side of eternity. Which leads me to ask about the spiritual dimensions of who I am. Better yet, let me ask you. What spiritual issues do you struggle with?

How do we strengthen our faith? Isn't it true that sometimes we talk a better game on Sunday than we actually manage to demonstrate Monday through Saturday? The contradictions we experience between what we express we believe and what we actually manage to integrate into the fabric of our daily lives is at times disturbing.

There are no quick fixes that promote spiritual well being. There is something about the importance of self-denial and living with an openness of servanthood and humility before God and others that has to serve as the driving motivation for the values and priorities we give to life in order for us to mature and develop as a person of faith. I have looked at all the quick fixes for life and been left wanting more. I am convinced that the problem goes deeper than giving people a few simple lifestyle adjustments and hoping all will be better. It is time to stop settling for business as usual. If we keep doing what we've always done, we'll keep getting what we've always gotten. Christ said, "Therefore, if anyone is in Christ, the new creation has come: The old has gone, the new is here!" (2 Corinthians 5:17). The biggest challenge comes with the mandate, "If anyone would come after me, he must deny himself and take up his cross and follow me" (Matthew 16:24). I don't know about you, but for me, that denotes change. It is not more of the same. If I want a different outcome, I have to do it differently.

Lesson three: Nothing is as important as the people in our lives. Build, maintain, and support relationships that honor God and promote their greatest good.

There is a thought-provoking chapter in one of Lloyd Ogilvie's books entitled *People Problems*. He tells about a sermon he preached at a church in Southern California. He described a well-scrubbed boy sitting with his parents in the front pew. Not once during the sermon did the youngster take his eyes off of Dr. Ogilvie. Dr. Ogilvie was immensely encouraged by his attention.

The theme of the sermon was centered on the idea that we are called not only to be Christ's friend, but in turn to be friends to others in his name. That included providing the gift of friendship to those who have hurt, disappointed, or frustrated us.

At the close of the sermon, Dr. Ogilvie extended an invitation for people to respond. He invited those who needed prayer for the healing of memories or the courage to be initiative agents of healing to people who distressed them. No one moved. The moments passed by in awkward silence.

Suddenly, the boy in the front row jumped to his feet. His mother attempted to retrieve him by grabbing at his jacket, but he was determined to respond to the invitation.

He hurried to the front and knelt at the alter rail. Placing his hands on the boy's shoulders, Dr. Ogilvie asked, "What do you want me to pray about?" Looking into Dr. Ogilvie's eyes, he said, "A couple of my friends have really been mean and hard on me. Please ask Jesus to help me be the kind of friend to them I wish they'd be to me."

As Dr. Ogilvie prayed that the boy would accept Jesus's friendship and have the courage to be a friend like Christ to his buddies who were troubling him, Dr. Ogilvie was overcome with emotion. Tears streamed down his face.

When he finished, the boy looked into Dr. Ogilvie's face and asked, "Why are you crying?"

Dr. Ogilvie responded, "That's the prayer I most need to pray too. Some of my friends have hurt me, and you've shown me that I need to forgive them and be their friend regardless of what they have done."

"Wow!" the boy exclaimed. "You'd better kneel down and ask Jesus to help you!" With that, he smiled and returned to his parents who were anxiously waiting for him in the front pew.

Dr. Ogilvie responded by walking to the other side of the kneeling rail as he glanced an appeal to the pastor of the church before he knelt for prayer. The pastor of the church heard his confession and desire to be healed, laid his hands on him, and prayed.

Dr. Ogilvie went back to his place behind the rail, repeated the invitation, and shared honestly what had just happened to him. That honest confession broke open the floodgate of God's power. Hundreds of people came forward for prayer. The Lord had used a young boy to touch the hearts of both the visiting preacher and the people.

I guess at times we all are troubled by people who contribute an abundance of stress in our lives. Face it, not everyone God places in our midst is easy to love. That doesn't negate the mandate that God's call on our life is to be loving.

There are some people you meet and intuitively you connect. You know immediately that you'd enjoy and value the gift of their friendship. At other times, you run across people who solicit a very different response.

Have you ever met anyone whose personality just grated on your nerves? We've all met people we'd just as soon avoid. In addition, perhaps even more disturbingly, folks who are true friends do or say things that create hurt or pain.

Dr. Ogilvie suggests that it is possible the Lord comes to us in the difficult people in our lives. He told us what we do for the hungry, the thirsty, the stranger, the naked and sick, the imprisoned, we do for him: "Whatever you did for one of the least of these brothers of mine, you did for me."

Could the same be true of people who trouble us? Have you ever stopped to think that how we respond to the needs of problem people may be our response to Christ?

About twelve years ago, I heard from a long-term friend that I'd known for fifteen or sixteen years. He and I don't always agree on theological issues, but his friendship is one that I value and appreciate. He is a brother in Christ.

My friend sent an e-mail in response to an article I had shared for his review. Let me say first, the article I sent for his reading was one that I had devoted somewhere between thirty to forty hours in writing. In the midst of that investment of time, from the beginning to the completion, I perceived that I experienced the Lord's leadership in chronicling the things I shared.

The article was extremely personal and included some of the highs and lows of my human and spiritual pilgrimage. It was an attempt on my part to be open and honest in reflecting back on my life and summing up some of the things that contribute to the person I am today. It was my hope that the reflections would glorify God.

My friend's response was one of bitter rebuke. From his perspective, what I had written was an abomination to the Lord. More disturbingly, his assessment based on what I had chronicled clearly demonstrated my living outside the framework of Christ's calling on my life. Ouch! It was pretty harsh. It actually said that what I had written was demonic rather than glorifying God.

It probably would add pizzazz to this article if I provided exact quotes. But truthfully, I ripped the printed copy I'd made for my files in a hundred pieces and threw it in the trash.

I was angry and hurt and indignant and mad! The list just went on and on. Oh, I forgot to add, furious. I was that too. I mumbled to myself something closely akin to "If my friend's brand of Christianity was all there was, it would be a dark day for folks in the midst of struggle looking for a lifeline." You'd have to be "spiritually psychotic" to satisfy all of his requirements. I could just hear Simon the Pharisee looking at what I had written and saying, "God I'm grateful that I'm not like this poor, ignorant, miserable wreck of a human being…"

When I ripped the printed copy of my friend's response into shreds and tossed it in the trash, it was as if I was saying, "Enough is enough. I'm finished with this!" (At some level, if I were to be painfully honest, I was also dismissing the value of the relationship.)

The symbolism of tearing up the harsh words he had written was paramount to distancing myself from his friendship. On a conscious level, I resolved it would be a very cold day before I sent another article for his review.

I was pretty smug in my resolve to call it quits with the communication. Then it dawned on me: my behavior was pretty reflective of that which had left me reeling. How was I responding to his command to turn the other cheek? Christ reminds us, "I demand that you love each other as much as I love you. And here is how to measure it. The greatest love is shown when a person lays down his life for his friends; and you are my friends if you obey me. I no longer call you slaves, for a master doesn't confide in his slaves; now you are my friends, provided by the fact that I have told you everything the Father told me" (John 15:12–15).

Oops! The ability to forgive and be a friend is his calling in my life. We can only do that with the Lord's help. When we avail ourselves to loving sacrificially, we find his strength can accomplish that in our lives.

Lesson four: Give priority to things that really matter.

We were standing for a congregational hymn at church. The person standing in front of me was wearing Levis. It was only a passing glance, but I caught sight of the label sewn on the back of his Levis that showed the waist size and length. I chuckled to myself when I realized the person standing in front of me was a foot more in circumference than the length of his Levis. I couldn't help but think, "I bet he'd prefer the order of the numbers were reversed or at least a little closer together."

A split second later, as I did the math in my head, I realized that people who live in glass houses shouldn't throw stones. The last time I bought slacks, mine were five inches more in circumference than in length. Would I prefer to reverse the order of those numbers? Absolutely!

There was a time in my young adulthood that my waist size was less than the length of my slacks. Unfortunately, that is no longer the case. Before the hymn concluded, I had the passing thought that it would take a great deal of effort, but with an exercise regime and lifestyle changes in my eating habits, I might be able to alter the numbers that would be reflected on my Levi size.

Later, as I reflected on reversing the order of my waist size and the length of my slacks, I recalled a story that John Claypool once told to illustrate a point. He told of a country pastor visiting in a church in Kentucky. The visiting pastor had come to church in a horse-drawn buggy. During the time for the Sunday night sermon, some of the boys skipped church and hurriedly switched the wheels on his buggy. They placed the little wheels in back and the larger wheels in front. Because of the long distance back to his home, the visiting pastor stayed overnight in the home of one of the deacons.

The next morning, the visiting pastor was outside looking very perplexed. When the deacon inquired what was wrong, the pastor responded that he was puzzled because the land was so flat. He had formed the distinct impression the previous night that they had traveled up a pretty steep incline.

The pastor and deacon walked around to the barn and discovered the switched wheels. The pastor laughingly said, "I guess when you get the big wheels where the little wheels should be and the little wheels where the big wheels should be, you wind up on the back of your neck."

Seems to me that there is a message in that. How often in life do we let happenstance and expectations dictate our priorities? How often do we get off-track, dealing with things of less significance instead of purposefully pursuing those things that promote spiritual growth and development?

Sadly, as a culture, we are probably more apt to spend time at the gym exercising and training in an attempt to alter the numbers on our Levis size than to purposefully and painstakingly invest in that which is eternal. Both require effort, however, only one has lasting significance.

Lesson five: Avoid the smugness of religious superiority. When it comes to our need for Christ, we are all on a level playing field.

When it comes to shopping, my wife can take an inordinate amount of time looking and relooking at any assortment of merchandise. On the other hand, I consider myself a consummate shopper. I know how to get in and out of a retail store in record speed.

For example, I have gotten the Pottery Barn route down to a two and one half minute overview. I generally walk through the store at a rapid pace. If I don't see a "sale" sign in my peripheral vision, I don't even slow down. I'm generally in and ready to be out of the store before my wife has turned the corner of the first aisle. Of course, she isn't as interested in the "sale" signs.

One Saturday morning, my wife conned me into going to several shops with her, including the Christian bookstore. As we were exiting the car, she said, "This should take just a minute." While she headed off in one direction, I browsed through the "recent release" section. I picked up Max Lucado's book *Traveling Light* and began gleaning through the pages. It took less than thirty seconds. I knew I wanted the book. I was then ready to go. As I looked up, my wife was nowhere in sight.

I looked down two or three more aisles and didn't see anything else that really drew my attention. I was ready to go, but my wife was still not in sight.

Looking for things to occupy my interest, I found myself standing in front of a display of Christian bumper stickers. My first thought was "You've got to be kidding." Personally, I'd never be caught driving a car with a Christian bumper sticker.

Standing before the display rack, I remembered a peer with whom I worked in the early 1970s. She drove a car with a bumper sticker that read: "In case of rapture, this car will be driverless." My friend was an animal lover. She had a dog and two cats and spent an inordinate amount of time wrestling with anxiety regarding who'd take care of her animals if she were taken away in the rapture.

In considering various options, she thought about a mutual friend of ours who lived eighty miles away. At that point in her life, our friend was not actively involved in attending a church. She was, however, actively involved in the animal rescue program in the county in which she resided. It didn't take much thought for my friend to come up with a solution to her pet problem. She would simply ask our mutual friend to drive eighty miles and pick up her pets for safekeeping.

I still remember being dismayed when I learned of the telephone conversation that resolved my friend's anxiety regarding provision for her animals.

Perhaps it was that same religious superiority mind-set that served as a backdrop for Jesus to tell the story of the pharisee and the tax collector. It was a parable for those who trusted in themselves and their religious superiority to gain favor with God. Of course, those with the pharisee's false sense of superiority were not only confident in their own righteousness, but they looked down on everybody else. They lived with a kind of contempt that considered other people to be irrelevant to God's calling on their life. Interestingly, Jesus told the story and twisted the predictable outcome. The religious hero of the day ultimately was described as the villain and the social and religious outcast became the hero.

I think Christ was attempting to highlight the truth that when it comes to our need for God's *grace*, we are all on a level playing field. The only honest assessment is one that responds, "God, be merciful to me, a sinner" (Luke 18:13). Self-satisfaction always falls short of securing that which only God can provide.

Early in Paul's Christian pilgrimage, he describes himself as "an apostle of the Lord Jesus Christ." Later, he reduced that claim to the "least among the apostles." Subsequently, he simply acknowledged he was "chief among sinners."

I don't know about you, but I'm not adding Christian bumper stickers to my vehicle. It is also my prayer that I'll avoid the pitfalls of Simon the Pharisee. Regrettably, I, too, like Paul, am chief among sinners. I'm grateful for God's *grace*.

Lesson six: Value the freedom and opportunities you've been provided by being an American.

Although it is not a dominant gene passed through my bloodline, for whatever reason, Craig, my son, prides himself on being a "great American hunter." I am not a hunter. Only a great American hunter would take two small children bear hunting in the dead of winter. At the time, he only had two children, ages two and three. He carried the three-year-old in a backpack. One of his hunting buddies assisted by carrying the two-year-old in a backpack. Seven years later, the bear is prominently displayed on a wall in their home. The two-year-old, who is now nine years of age, regularly invites new children in the neighborhood to come inside and see the bear he killed with his father's help.

Who else would orchestrate playtime for his children by spending hours with them reloading bullets and teaching them the precise details associated with the skill? It baffles my imagination that both children wanted camouflage clothing for Christmas. I couldn't help but wonder, "What kind of redneck children are they becoming?"

Even more puzzling, my son won't let his children have toy guns. He wants them to know that guns are real and that they have a purpose. They are not toys. Despite his ban on toy guns, several years ago, Craig was amused one evening when he got home and found his son, William, playing with a toy gun. He had fashioned the gun himself by configuring attachments from the vacuum cleaner. Craig said William's creation actually resembled a gun. William couldn't have been more pleased with himself. He was three years old at the time. After hearing William's make-shift gun story, my mind wandered back to my childhood years. Although I had no frame of reference for real weapons during my childhood years because my Dad had "enough of guns" during the war, my brothers and I had an arsenal of toy guns in our preschool and elementary school years. Playing "cowboys and Indians" was a favorite pastime. Eventually, that activity gave way to playing "soldiers."

There was no way to go to the movie and see *To Hell and Back* depicting the life of Audie Murphy, a decorated war hero of WW II, and not want to pretend to be a war hero. My brothers and I spent hours absorbed in all the activities of war. We carried toy M1 rifles, gave and received orders, dug foxholes in the backyard, and took turns being the "General." (Note: I really did enjoy giving orders!). Those childhood memories are as real today as they were sixty-plus years ago in the midst of the experience. It was a game of "childhood fun."

As we grew older, we outgrew the play activity without acquiring any real comprehension that "freedom isn't free." The "threat of freedom" or the notion of "the real implications of war" was not a concept for which we had any firsthand knowledge.

We knew that we were privileged to be Americans and live in a land where we enjoyed freedom. We learned that as children because we grew up having that communicated to us by our parents, our extended family, our teachers, and our church. From our childhood frame of reference, we got the message, but it was only in theory; we didn't have any firsthand experience to go along with it.

The peril of freedom that manifests itself in "life and death" situations is always an abrupt reality that clearly drives home the message that "freedom isn't free." There are insurmountable costs associated with the pursuit of freedom.

Shortly before my brother's plane went down in Vietnam, the aircraft of two of his best friends exploded in flight after being hit by a surface-to-air missile. There was no way either of the two men on board escaped. Predictably, the experience was a despairing "coming of age" experience for my brother as he learned firsthand that "freedom isn't free."

Four decades later, as I've observed my son, nephew, and others invest their lives in ensuring our continued freedom, I have such a high regard for those who serve our country in that capacity. I recognize that freedom isn't free. It comes as a result of sacrifice.

We are so blessed to live in a land where we enjoy the privileges and opportunities afforded us as Americans. The debt of gratitude for and to those who entrust their fate to whatever it takes to protect our country, coupled with the bountiful "hand of God" who has protected, blessed, and provided unprecedented opportunities is nothing short of remarkable.

Every time we see an American flag waving in the breeze, our hearts and heads should offer a prayer of thanksgiving for the privileges afforded us. I like the way Lee Greenwood expressed it in his song "God Bless the USA":

> If tomorrow all the things were gone
> I'd worked for all my life,
> And I had to start again
> with just my children and my wife.
> I'd thank my lucky stars to be living here today,
> 'Cause the flag still stands for freedom
> and they can't take that away.
>
> And I'm proud to be an American
> where at least I know I'm free.
> And I won't forget the men who died,
> who gave that right to me.
> And I'd gladly stand up next to you
> and defend her still today.
> 'Cause there ain't no doubt I love this land
> God bless the USA
>
> From the lakes of Minnesota, to the hills of Tennessee,
> across the plains of Texas, from sea to shining sea,
>
> From Detroit down to Houston and New York to LA,
> Well, there's pride in every American heart,
> and it's time to stand and say:
>
> I'm proud to be an American
> where at least I know I'm free.

And I won't forget the men who died,
who gave that right to me.
And I'd gladly stand up next to you
and defend her still today.
'Cause there ain't no doubt I love this land
God bless the USA."

Lesson seven: Make room in your life for divine intervention. God doesn't always adhere to logic and human understanding.

Winter before last was very different from this winter. In contrast, it was very cold. I remember that I was bundled up attempting to stay warm on a Saturday morning while doing my best to repair a broken waterline outside my home. I had previously wrapped all the outside pipes, but the cold was no respecter of persons.

I am not a plumber. When I discovered the broken water pipe in my front yard, my initial thought was to call for help. Since it was very early on a Saturday morning, I dismissed the thought with the notion that it would be a good opportunity for me to increase my skill set. I could repair it myself.

I went to the well house and turned the water off. Within thirty minutes, I was standing with a crowd of other people on aisle nine at Home Depot looking for repair parts. Apparently, mine was not the only broken waterline in the area. It added to the notion that misery loves company.

A short time later, the broken waterline had been spliced and everything appeared to be in order. In two hours, I could turn the water back on, and life as I've known it would be restored. Actually, what I discovered two hours later is that I didn't cut enough of the broken waterline off before making my repair. There was still a hairline crack in the waterline and a fine stream of water was spraying out the side of the pipe.

Hey, what's one more trip to Home Depot? This time, there were even more people on aisle nine. Not a problem. I even simplified the process this time and decided to thread and tighten

the faucet into the connection before making the splice and glu-
ing it on.

Unfortunately, the faucet didn't thread correctly in the connection. After two turns by hand, it was obvious that it wasn't
threaded correctly. I took it out, put it in, took it out, put it in. It
looked right, but it didn't feel right. Not wanting to go back to
Home Depot, I relied on brute force and a pair of channel locks
to tighten the faucet. I was really proud of myself. The connection
was tight.

Two hours later after the glue dried, I turned the water back
on. The discovery was unbelievable: *Drip, drip, drip!* Obviously
the tight connection wasn't fail proof. I stood there watching the
faucet drip and had the passing thought that I should pray for
God's help with the faucet. I was conscious of the thought—
the spirit leads us to know how we should pray. I quickly dismissed that thought with the notion that I wouldn't insult God
with that request. The *drip, drip, drip* was my own fault. It didn't
help that my wife suggested I put a bucket under the faucet to
catch the water and use it to water plants. Instead I went back to
Home Depot.

I even bought a new faucet this time. I wasn't going to take
any chances. At least I didn't have to spend much time looking for
what I needed. I was very familiar with aisle nine at Home Depot.

After wrapping plumber's tape around the new faucet, I took
the new connection to be spliced out of the bag. Immediately, I
recognized that somehow I had picked up the wrong size connection. It was not what I needed! Haste makes waste. How could I
be so stupid? There were two absolutes that immediately came to
mind: I was *not* going back to Home Depot that day and I was
not putting a bucket under the connection to catch the water.
Enough said, I called it a day.

Shortly before bedtime, I turned on the porch light and walked
outside with the dog. I glanced in the direction of the water faucet. I was shocked by what I saw. Closer inspection revealed that

it was no longer dripping. I even had the passing thought, did I turn the water back off at the pump? No, I had not, but the *drip, drip, drip* was gone.

As I drifted off to sleep that night, I had the sense that God was saying, "I told you to ask me for help. You didn't, but since I'm your friend, I helped you anyway." It has been a year. The water line is still not dripping. Obviously God makes house calls, and he is an incredible friend.

If there is a truth to be learned, it is simply that things turn out better when we rely on the friendship of God to meet our needs. I can think of no better lesson to negotiate life. It really is more than enough.

THE DOS EQUIS MAN

AT THE RISK of sharing a character flaw (I will probably live to regret this)…At the risk of sharing a character flaw, I've got to tell you, every time I hear one of those Dos Equis commercials about "the most interesting man in the world," I get a little envious. You know the commercials, they always conclude with Jonathan Goldsmith talking. He is the man with the Spanish accent who says at the end of each spot, "I don't always drink beer, but when I do, I prefer Dos Equis." Just for the record, that is not what makes me envious.

It is the characteristics of the most interesting man in the world that catch my attention:

- At museums, he's allowed to touch the art.
- His blood smells like cologne.
- Sharks have a week dedicated to him.
- He once had an awkward moment, just to see how it feels.
- The police often question him, just because they find him interesting.

- He is the most interesting man in the world.

I recently had lunch with a friend who lives a very different kind of life than I do. He may not be the Dos Equis man, but his life is interesting. He is a guy in his mid-to-late thirties. He and his best friend started their own company right out of college. It was in the computer-related industry. They subsequently sold that company and ventured on to something else. At some point, while he and his business partner were between business ventures, he went to work for another company. That all changed shortly after he took his son to work with him. His son had a great time. At the end of the day, his son said to him, "Dad, when I grow up, I want to be just like you. I want to work here."

That was all the impetus he needed to take the risk of resigning his job and following his dreams. He wanted something better for his son. Actually, he wanted something better for himself. He decided to follow his heart. He and his business partner started a management training/consultation firm. They didn't ask anyone how to do it. They just followed their passion and put it together in a way that made sense to them. They have been highly successful. Today they provide high-end, high-dollar training all over the world. They have provided pro bono training for our agency. I know firsthand from attending the training that they are incredibly skilled. They create success.

I guess at some level, all of us want to be successful. How that plays itself out in our life depends on personal interests and motivation. We each want to be highly regarded and seen as a person of value to our family, work, church, and community.

At some level, I probably give too much credence to what other people think. For example, I often present training information at conferences, workshops, or other in-service training venues. Following my presentation, I generally have some sense of whether or not I've connected with the class and whether the information shared was of value. I don't need to review written evaluations to have some sense of whether the training was successful. However, if offered an opportunity to thumb through written evaluations, I always do so. Without fail, I can thumb through a handful of evaluations reflecting scores with the highest possible rating and notice one that indicated the training was marginal, uninteresting, misrepresented, etc. It is almost like the default button in my brain automatically discounts the handful of positive responses and focuses entirely on the one that provides the negative rating.

Why is that? Some time ago, I was in Fort Worth for a meeting. I arrived about an hour early and decided to take advantage of the extra free time. Looking at my watch and then inventorying businesses in the neighboring shopping center, it didn't take me long to chart my course. It appeared there were only two places open that time of the morning. One was a grocery store and the other a bookstore. It didn't seem like a tough choice to make. I made a beeline to the bookstore.

As I was scanning the books in the psychology section, I stumbled across a book entitled *Too Soon Old, Too Late Smart*. I eagerly picked it up. The title sounded like a biographical overview of my life. As the day turned out, it could have been the voice of prophecy. They say ignorance is bliss, but I certainly didn't anticipate such a drastic plunge in the stock market. Too soon old-too late smart—story of my life.

Too Soon Old, Too Late Smart was actually written by a psychiatrist. It was an attempt to offer the benefit of his professional observations across thirty years of practice that seemed applicable to a myriad of folks coming for psychiatric help. In a kind of "one size fits all" descriptor, he chronicled observations or advice that almost anyone could benefit from.

One of the chapters that caught my attention was entitled "The Statute of Limitations on Your Childhood Has Expired." Across thirty years of practice, the author counseled adults of all ages who credited their continuing failures, their inabilities to successfully negotiate relationships, their ongoing lack of self-esteem, and the sense that "I can't cope" to scars left over from childhood.

Fortunately for me, after five and a half decades, I have mostly made peace with not being selected for the First State Bank Little League baseball team at the age of nine. In the process, I am also grateful that in many ways I am still very much in touch with the little boy living inside me. I give him permission to show up at every occasion and focus simply on having fun and enjoying life. He's a nice kid. You'd like him. Most people do.

The kid inside me is also grateful that the old man he hangs out with is no longer judged or evaluated by athletic ability or prowess. The lyrics from "Don't Laugh at Me" fall pretty close to home: "I'm that kid on every playground who is always chosen last…" I'm in a different peer group now. My worth and ability is no longer determined in part by how well I play the game. My only job is to show up. His power is made perfect in weakness.

I want to be successful. I am not delusional. I will never be a contender for being the Dos Equis man. No one would be tempted to define me as the most interesting man in the world.

I recently participated in a training session with about forty people. In an effort to get acquainted, we were told, "Introduce yourself. Tell us who you are and what you do." After sixty-plus years I've gotten the name down. I go by Don. It's not Donald, it's not Donnie—it's Don. If you spell it backward, it is nod, a sign of agreement or of falling asleep.

What I do may not be any more complicated than my name, but I haven't worked out all the kinks in the description. When you work with people, you never know what a day can bring. Generally, when someone asks what I do, I simply say, "I do the best I can. That's my story and I'm sticking to it."

Despite the fact that I'm not articulate enough to describe what I do, I really like what I do. That's not to say I am a stranger to "job-related stress," but given the choice of retiring tomorrow and being relegated to sitting on the back porch or going to work, I'd opt to go to work, primarily because I have fun in that environment.

On a Friday evening about a year ago, I attended a concert at a large church in Houston. The church was hosting the concert featuring their choir with the accompaniment of a world-renowned pianist. They dedicated the performance as a benefit for the program I am associated with in Houston.

The concert was scheduled to start at 7:30 p.m. I arrived a few minutes early and was told by the person handling the schedule, "The program is going to be a longer program than we anticipated. I think it will be two hours, but with that said, I think it is important that you have an opportunity to speak at the end. It is okay to be brief, but we'd really like to hear from you."

I'm glad I took my blood pressure pill that morning because my anxiety level immediately rose significantly. No one had mentioned earlier that I would be provided an opportunity to speak. I don't mind public speaking, but I am not good at impromptu speaking. I much prefer to have an opportunity to carefully craft my thoughts on paper before I speak.

I have to say, the concert was incredible. There were probably at least 150 people in the choir, and I think I could safely say a thousand people were in attendance. I alternated from feeling like a kid in a candy store to a kid going to big church for the first time. It was awe-inspiring to hear the music, but the closer we got to the end of the program, the higher my anxiety level seemed to be related to the opportunity to speak. Even though I was told it was okay to be brief, I at least wanted to share something meaningful.

I can't tell you anything about the last two songs that were presented before I walked up on stage. Without pen and paper, I attempted to craft something meaningful to share in my head. The challenge would be in remembering it.

Fortunately, when I began to speak, my thoughts were coherent and my anxiety disappeared. When I finally made my way back to my seat, I was greatly relieved. I had the sense that my comments were well received and that I had shared something substantive.

A few minutes later, I was standing next to my brother-in-law in the foyer of the church. He and my sister-in-law live in Houston, and they attended the concert with us. Our wives had gone across the foyer to purchase a CD of the guest pianist. While we were waiting, my brother-in-law leaned over and said, "Don, I was a little surprised by your comments at the conclusion of the concert. It ended pretty abruptly. I was really expecting something a little more polished. You probably need to work on that."

Initially, I was speechless. I finally managed to say, "If you have some pointers that could help me, I'd really appreciate your feedback. It really is important to me that I get it right. What could I have done differently?"

He broke into laughter and said, "I'm only joking. You were amazing. You just walked up there, took the microphone, and just started talking. You were so calm, and it all seemed so well-planned."

For a startling instant before my brother-in-law told me he was "only joking," I had a flashback and was once again that nine-year-old kid who didn't make the First State Bank Little League team. Funny, isn't it, how scripts from the past can be haunting? Well, maybe not so funny!

On a conscious level, I have the cognitive ability to know that my value and worth isn't based on my performance. On an emotional level, I don't always manage to connect the dots that quickly. Perhaps one of the reasons that I say, tongue in cheek, that I am envious of the Dos Equis man is that his abilities are never questioned:

- At museums, he's allowed to touch the art.
- His blood smells like cologne.
- Sharks have a week dedicated to him.
- He once had an awkward moment, just to see how it feels.

- The police often question him, just because they find him interesting.
- He is the most interesting man in the world.

This side of eternity none of us come equipped with all those features. When it comes to our humanity, we all stand in need of that which only God can provide. "For all have sinned and come short of the glory of God" (Romans 3:23). Despite the brokenness and inadequacies that represent the common denominators of our lives, we are loved by God. He offers the gift of redemption and restoration. That is more than enough.

FAMILY TIES

ON ALMOST A daily basis, I am reminded that we live in a very troubled world, and relationally, we are prone to problems. Honestly, I never cease to be amazed at the level of pain and hurt we are capable of inflicting on those we should love most.

Several weeks ago, I had a strange conversation with a woman from out of town. She had initially called me on a Friday evening to request information related to possible placement for her four-teen-year-old-son. Someone had told her that the boy's ranch program our agency operates might be an appropriate placement resource. Since I am not the person who makes placement decisions, I provided her the contact information she needed to talk with the appropriate person.

The following Monday evening, I missed a telephone call from her. I didn't find the voice message she left until Tuesday morning. The voice message stated, "Please call me immediately when you get this message." Her voice tone was gruff. I had the sense that she was not happy.

When I reached her by phone, I was surprised. She couldn't have been more pleasant. "Thank you for returning my call. The boy's ranch program didn't have any openings. Do you work with other residential programs that might be a possibility?"

In discussing some other options with her, she mentioned by happenstance that her son is adamant that he is not going anywhere. I responded that she needed to talk with him about placement. He would have to be willing to be admitted before we'd consider being a resource for him. We don't hold kids hostage.

She was very surprised by that. "What? If he isn't willing to come, you won't just send staff out to my home and forcibly take him away? My ex-husband has talked to a place that is willing to accept him. They will come to my home and forcibly take my son with them. The problem with that placement is the conditions my ex-husband has set for me in order for him to assume the financial responsibility. He is very wealthy, but in order for him to assume responsibility, he is mandating that I have to sign forms relinquishing my parental rights and agree to have no further contact with my son for the remainder of his childhood. He will have the papers filed in court. He says he will have me thrown in jail if I make any attempt to have contact with him."

My only response was to ask the question, "Why would you want to do that?"

She answered, "I'm so tired of dealing with him, but I really don't want to do that. I don't want to relinquish my parental rights and be totally out of his life."

I was confused. I thought maybe the father was offering his home to his son. I asked, "If you do that, will your ex-husband allow your son to live with him?"

"Oh no, he doesn't want him. He is going to place him. He just wants me totally out of the picture."

At the risk of you knowing that I sometimes default to manipulation through guilt, I replied, "I've got to be honest with you. I am obviously missing something. Help me understand how you think it would be in your son's best interest to have no contact with you for the next four years?" She immediately answered, "I don't think that it would be."

"Then why would you consider it? You are the only mother your son is ever going to have. What message does it give him if you choose to take that course of action? You may be sick and tired of his behavior, but that doesn't mean you don't love him, does it?"

"Absolutely not! Thank you! Thank you. Thank you. You've helped me make a decision. I'm not going to do that. I think God must be responsible for this telephone call."

Shouldn't the importance of relationships be the primary focus of our lives? The economy of our nation no longer places value on relationships. Sadly, I predict we are in the midst of what may prove to be the most debilitating epidemic we've known—the epidemic of loneliness.

Sometimes even those who seemingly have successfully embraced life routinely eliminate others because they simply don't have the time. There are places to go, things to do, deadlines to meet, and the concept of importance of shared time with others fails to even register as something that should be given importance.

In one of John Ortberg's books, he makes the statement: "Hurried people cannot love." He credits Lewis Grant with suggesting that we are "afflicted with 'sunset fatigue.' When we come home at the end of a day's work, those who need our love the most, those to whom we are most committed, end up getting the leftovers. Sunset fatigue is when we are just too tired, or too drained, or too preoccupied, to love the people to whom we have made the deepest promises."

On top of that, have you given thought to the impact of technology on children? Most ten-year-olds can navigate through my iPad without having to think twice, but what do they know about friendship development, social skills, conflict resolution, and the joys associated with sharing life with others? As a value system, we don't give priority to the concept.

One of the old photographs on display in my home is a picture taken on Christmas Eve 1904. It is a picture of my grandmother's family. My grandmother is included in the photograph along with twenty-seven other family members. It is one of several photographs of my grandmother's family that I now have in my possession. They were all taken at different times across the span of many years. I have always heard that "a picture is worth a thousand words." These seem to highlight the importance of family and the importance of connection.

The effort taken for inclusion in an extended family photo in 1904 differs fairly dramatically from today because of the ease of transportation we have available to us. It is easier to get the family together now than it was in the "horse and buggy" era, which makes me think that our grandparents knew more about the importance of family and ongoing connections than does the current generation.

I recently read that the average household in America is comprised of three people. Perhaps it is because we are so transitory, but we have evolved into a society that no longer appears to value or support extended family connections. We mostly value our privacy and manage to fill our time with things other than relationship-building and connectedness. We have allowed technology to fill our lives with gadgets, television, computers, video games, and other things that consume our time and steal from us the simple joy and value of sharing time with others.

The thing I find most disturbing about this trend is the long-term deficits that will impact the children of today. Relationships don't just happen. It takes effort and skill to know how to communicate, express our needs, have a voice, negotiate compromise, and extend ourselves to have the capacity to simply provide unconditional love to others. Without repetitive opportunities to practice those skills, the portions of our brain that makes us relational creatures will fail to fully develop.

Another thing I find disturbing is the lack of adults readily available to support and impact the lives of today's children. Children need cheerleaders. They need role models. They need mentors. They need to know they are important. They need to know they are loved.

Research makes it clear that children who have at least five significant adults in their lives fare much better at being equipped for life when they reach adulthood than those who don't have that level of support.

I enjoy listening to music. I am particularly fond of Neil Diamond's music, despite the fact that some content highlights the isolation and loneliness of our existence. One of my favorite examples is the lyrics to "I Am I Said":

> LA's fine, the sun shines most the time
> The feeling is laid-back
> Palm trees grow and the rents are low
> But you know I keep thinking about
> Making my way back
>
> Well, I'm New York City born and raised
> But nowadays, I'm lost between two shores
> LA's fine, but it ain't home
> New York's home but it ain't mine no more
>
> I am, I said
> To no one there
> And no one heard at all
> Not even the chair
> I am, I cried
> I am, said I
> And I am lost, and I can't even say why
> Leavin' me lonely still
>
> Did you ever read about a frog who dreamed of being a king
> And then became one
> Well, except for the names and a few other changes
> If you talk about me, the story's the same one

But I got an emptiness deep inside
And I've tried but it won't let me go
And I'm not a man who likes to swear
But I've never cared for the sound of being alone

I am, I said
To no one there
And no one heard at all
Not even the chair
I am, I cried
I am, said I
And I am lost, and I can't even say why

I am, I said
I am, I cried
I am...

In Tom Brokaw's book, *The Greatest Generation*, he claims, perhaps accurately, that the World War II generation is in many ways the greatest in American history. He has an entire section titled "Love, Marriage and Commitment," which begins,

> The World War II generation shares so many common values: duty, honor, country, personal responsibility and the marriage vow, "For better or worse..." It was the last generation in which, broadly speaking, marriage was a commitment and divorce was not an option...Of all the new marriages in 1940, one in six ended in divorce. By the late 1990's, that number was one in two.

"And they lived happily ever after" is certainly not the experience of many couples in today's world. How many people do you know who've been married multiple times? Doesn't it surprise you how often relationships dissolve and almost before the legal entanglement is resolved, many have moved on to another relationship and another life?

I can't begin to even imagine managing the emotional upheaval of a house divided and torn apart. I'm just not that resilient. I jokingly tell people that if my wife had murdered me when she first thought about it, she'd be out of prison by now. That has to be a bittersweet awareness.

Seriously, I can't think of many things more disturbing than dissolution of a family, particularly when children are involved. I've spent enough years working with children scarred by the aftermath of their parents' divorce to know that there has to be a better problem-solving solution.

There is ongoing pain associated with the brokenness of a home divided. I observed it firsthand. A shroud of civility cloaked their conversation. Had I not been present to witness the interaction, observe the body language, and sense the degree of pain being experienced by both estranged parents, I would have missed the unspoken agony associated with a question as mundane as "What are your plans for the holiday?"

The fact that one parent was "planning" without coordination or consideration of the other meant that subsequently one parent would not be sharing the holiday with their child. Sadly, both parents, for the first time since they had promised years earlier: "Till death do us part," would experience the holiday in a stupor of regret and bewilderment wondering how something so disruptive and painful could happen in their home.

It was by happenstance that I stumbled into the conversation, but it left me feeling saddened and ineffective to say or do anything that could orchestrate a more positive outcome. Most of all, I hurt for their child who was still too young to comprehend the concept of "irreconcilable differences." This year for the first time, she would not be sharing the holiday with both parents. It all seemed surreal and unfair.

During holiday times, while many are caught up in the activities associated with enjoyment, many don't find that to be their experience. For them, "merriment" and "wonder" are not the overriding considerations of the holiday season. While their holiday plans may still be ill-defined, the broad parameters are already settled. The divorce decree assigns one parent or the other access to their child during the holiday.

Sharing and coordinating schedules for children of divorced parents takes an inordinate amount of effort and communication between parents who may not have parted all that amicably. Unfortunately, too often, children are shuffled between households in a manner that negates their best interest and emotional well-being. One parent or the other seemingly goes out of their way to make parental visitation for the other parent difficult and stressful. Children are used as pawns to "heap coals of fire" on the other parent without consideration of the subtle aversive emotional toll the interchange takes on the children who are involved.

The best gift parents who share children and live in separate households can provide their child is the freedom to be unencumbered with the stress associated with holiday planning and time-sharing. It is not an easy task. It takes an awareness of God's love and a yield to his leadership to successfully pull that off. When that can happen it is more than enough.

FAILURE TO PAY ATTENTION

THREE YEARS AGO, my younger brother and I were in our hometown for the funeral of an uncle. At some point during the second day of our visit, my brother said, "Don, it's been really nice spending time with you. You and I are just alike. My family says it's true of me, but it's also true of you.

"They say that most of the time, I am in a fog. They think I am oblivious to what's happening around me. I don't really think that's true of me, but it is so obviously true of you. It kind of tickles me to see it manifest before my very eyes. Maybe I see what they are talking about."

I am consistently hesitant to acknowledge there are times when I am totally oblivious to what's going on. However, on an ongoing basis, my wife gently redirects me by saying I am not paying attention. She thinks my brother is right about me being in a fog most of the time. She also thinks it is equally true of my brother as well.

At any rate, I'd never be purposefully insensitive. Never ever in a thousand years would I have stopped to consider that Valentine's Day poses a problem for some people. After all—the Valentine card exchange thing—didn't that end with elementary school?

My wife doesn't need a card from me to know that I love her. I take out the trash on a regular basis to communicate that, and she is far too practical to want me to spend money on flowers that fade too quickly or chocolate that could mess up her healthy eating trend. Perhaps I've got it covered for this year.

I remember walking into the cubicle office of a colleague at work just before Valentine's Day. The lady in the adjacent cubicle warned me not to go in because "she's in a bad mood." I didn't even bother to slow down.

Meeting the challenge head on and knowing the warning given me had been overheard, I simply rounded the corner and asked, "What's the problem?"

The response caught me off guard. "I'm sick and tired of being alone. Valentine's Day is next week and I have no one. I'm tired of being single. I want a husband."

Don't ever think I can't think on my feet. I casually suggested that she might check with dial a prayer—that's 1-800-dialaprayer.

Her response was immediate. "I have prayed—I've prayed for a very long time. I'm tired of waiting." I countered that she was forgetting that a day can be as a thousand years to God and suggested that she might be rushing things. In an attempt to be serious, I reminded her that it takes being a friend in order to have a friend. Perhaps she should start there. I cautioned her to slow down. After all, kindness grows.

It was a strange conversation. I almost suggested she write to Dr. Phil. Instead I promised to put her on my prayer list.

I turned around and the person who had cautioned me to steer clear was standing in the hallway. She had overheard our entire conversation.

"I want one too," she said.

"One what?" I asked.

"Oh, not a husband. I'd start with just a date," she replied.

The next day, I announced to both ladies that I'd figured it out. They needed to partner with the US Marine Corps because they too were looking for a few good men. Neither colleague thought my suggestion was as funny as I did. Maybe my brother is right. I can be insensitive. Perhaps I do live in a fog.

John Ortberg expresses it this way, "There is no tragedy like the tragedy of the unopened gift." Garrison Keillor tells a story, called "A Day in the Life of Clarence Bunsen," about an older man who realizes the years have slipped away and his life has missed something.

> Clarence goes to see Father Emil at Our Lady of Perpetual Responsibility for some advice. Normally Clarence goes to the Lutheran church, but he wants a second opinion. When that doesn't help, he walks past his old school and climbs the hill overlooking Lake Wobegon, where he and his friends played as kids years ago.
>
> While he is reflecting on his life, Clarence hears some kids coming up the path. For some strange reason he runs ahead of them and climbs an old tree he remembers from childhood. The kids stop right under his tree; they know he's around somewhere but don't think to look up. Clarence knew that if he dropped down on them or even yelled, 'Ha!' they would jump out of their shoes. He watches them, so full of excitement and life, and thinks to himself, *I wish I could be like that. I just seem to go through life with my eyes closed and my ears shut. People talk to me, and I don't even hear them. Whole days go by, and I can't remember what happened. The woman I've lived with for thirty-six years, if you asked me to describe her, I'd have to stop and think about it. It's like I've lived half my life waiting for my life to begin, thinking it's somewhere off in the future. And now I'm thinking about death all the time. It's time to live, to wake up and do something.*

Was my brother right? Is it really true that I walk around in a fog most of the time? If it is true, I am obviously in denial. Yet despite my ongoing perception that I'm very alert, focused, and keenly aware of my circumstances, I do have to acknowledge that on occasion I may appear to be in a fog.

It wasn't that long after my conversation with my brother that I needed to mail a letter. Because of the size of the correspondence, I knew it would require special postage. A first-class stamp would not cover the cost. Since I needed to drive into town, I opted to stop by the new post office. Rumor had it that it was now open. The old post office had been small and antiquated. In addition, I didn't always have the impression that the employees who worked behind the counter really liked their job. I routinely avoided going to that post office in the town where I lived for that reason.

The new post office was a much larger building and located on the highway through town. It was an attractive building fashioned out of white limestone. I had wanted to go inside and look around, but I had never driven by during business hours. Since it was now open for business and I was in the area, needing to mail a letter gave me a great opportunity.

I was incredibly impressed when I walked through the front door. I'd never seen a post office like this one. There was even a lobby area with what appeared to be an expensive looking oriental rug and comfortable chairs. "Wow! Wow! Wow!" Those were the three words that immediately came to mind.

I was also surprised to recognize the employee behind the counter. I had no idea she worked for the post office. When I saw her last, she was working at a convenience store where I sometimes stopped for coffee. Since no one else was at the counter, I verbalized from across the room how impressed I was with the new look and made some statement that I'd never seen a post office anywhere as nice as this one.

Handing her my letter, I explained that I thought it would require more than a first-class stamp. She took the letter from my hand and said, "You are right. This weighs too much for a first-class stamp." Her next words caught me by surprise. "We don't sell postage here. You will need to go next door to the post office. This is the bank."

No sooner than the words were out of her mouth, I sensed that eyes from any number of people looking out of their offices were focused on me. How could I have made such a mistake? Maybe I was in a fog. It obviously was not the first time nor the last.

Shortly after moving back to the Austin area, I made the discovery that in the early morning darkness, one intersection can look very much like another. I was obviously lost in thought one morning as I made my way to work. My wife would say, "I wasn't paying attention." I don't recall what I was thinking about, but I do recall being surprised when I discovered the intersection for my left-hand turn was only a few yards in front of me. Fortunately, I was in the left lane and was able to quickly negotiate moving over to the left-hand turn lane.

As I did so, I noticed the continuous stream of headlights making their way past me in the other direction. It was a non-stop continuous caravan of vehicles. They were all moving at a high rate of speed. I was grateful that eventually there would be a left-hand turn arrow. Without that assistance, I'd never be able to negotiate the turn.

I also looked to my left, and as far as I could see, there was a continuous line of cars waiting to turn right on the roadway I was exiting. I had the passing thought that I was glad my commute was almost completed. I'd hate to be starting out with the level of traffic I was currently experiencing.

While I was processing the traffic congestion, I made the sad realization that I was turning at the wrong intersection. No wonder it seemed like my time to turn came quickly. I had no idea where the road I was turning on would eventually lead.

Despite the realization that I did not want to turn, the die was cast, I had no way out. The cars going by me on the right precluded my moving back into the other lane of traffic. Making the wrong turn was a costly expenditure of time. I did eventually make it to work, but it was not anywhere close to a direct route. For a while, I wasn't sure where I'd wind up.

Later that day, as I was returning home, it occurred to me that despite my best intent, I sometimes easily become distracted and take a wrong turn. Often in the process, I misplace priorities and goals that ought to be more reflective of what I ultimately hope to accomplish. At times, it is beneficial to evaluate where we really are in our human and spiritual pilgrimage. If we continue on the course we are now taking, will we fulfill our personal goals and invest in that which has eternal significance?

Wrong turns have a tendency to lead to other wrong turns. If we continue with the priorities we currently embrace, where will our life take us? Is that what we really want to accomplish? Are there times we need to take a U-turn and get back on course?

Several years ago, I narrowly escaped learning that lesson the hard way. We were on vacation and had toured the lost city of Pompeii, returning to the cruise ship about four hours before our ship was set to depart from Sorrento, Italy. I don't know if it is just that I have "stupid" tattooed on my forehead, but I've never been one to let a "big adventure" (actually any kind of adventure) go unexplored. A friend told me once that during his growing-up years, his mother often counseled him by saying, "When you find yourself in the middle of one of life's big adventures, just remember you had other options. You could have been safely at home in bed."

At any rate, I decided to take advantage of the opportunity to explore Sorrento. I did that knowing clearly that "time waits for no man"—neither does a cruise ship. But it was a full four hours before the ship was set to leave the harbor.

I'm probably exaggerating, but it felt like it only took five minutes to walk from the harbor up the five hundred feet to the main level of the city. Actually, I stopped briefly halfway up to catch my breath. It was like taking the stairs to the top of a fifty-story building.

When I reached the top of the stairs and gave a sigh of relief that I was finally on street level, I had no idea where I was in proximity to the town square of the city. I've always considered myself "directionally astute," so I headed in the direction that I thought "felt right."

After going a couple of very long blocks, it appeared to me that nothing looked familiar. We had been by the city square on the tour bus that took us to Pompeii. Consequently, I opted to take the next right turn and walk that direction for a while. The thing that I discovered was that the streets didn't follow a rectangular pattern. The next turn left me no closer to emerging near the city square than any of my previous efforts. I glanced at my watch. I'd only been walking thirty-five minutes. I didn't have to worry, I'd eventually find my way.

One wrong turn led to another. Soon I was out of the shopping area of the city and in the residential area. The streets were narrower. I found myself wanting to keep going in order to get some sense of the architecture. Most of the structures were multi-stories and included balconies covered with plants. It was very picturesque.

After providing ample time to "get a feel" for the landscape and residential area, I then attempted to backtrack my steps and once again try to locate the square of the city.

After about an hour and a half of walking without coming any closer to locating the square or even sight of the harbor, I was becoming a little anxious. My wife had suggested that I take five Euros with me when I went for my walk. What I was beginning to realize is that five Euros wouldn't even get me a bus ride back to the harbor. (I said I was a little anxious. I was very anxious. The ship was leaving in two hours. I was clueless to know how to find it. I had no passport or any other form of identification with me.)

I was now confident that I needed something other than my ability to be "directionally astute" to help me find my way back to the harbor. I stopped a couple of people on the street and asked for directions. That in and of itself was a challenge. I don't speak Italian—well, I do know how to say "Mamma Mia" and move my hands, but that falls short of "How do I get back to the harbor?"

Eventually, I found someone who spoke English and they provided the directions I needed. As I made my journey back following directions, I was amazed at how far I had walked. I also determined that I am not as "directionally astute" as I'd like to think.

Once the ship was in sight, I'm sure my blood pressure dropped significantly. I still had my five Euros. I also resolved that the next time I took a self-paced excursion, I'd take more cash.

At some level, I have to admit that my wife is at times perceptive when she makes the assessment that I don't pay attention.

I have jokingly told my wife on a number of occasions that we need to travel while we are still young enough to drive at night. However, I guess you are never too old to learn. Our recent adventure into Canada underscored the importance of more than night vision.

To begin with, we barely made it to the airport for an early Saturday morning flight. The roadway was under construction, and it was a major traffic jam. Nothing was moving. I am not exaggerating. We sat in the same spot for fifteen minutes and didn't move an inch. Finally I came to the realization that we were going to miss our flight.

It was a first for me, but I made an illegal U-turn across the median and took another route. We made it to the airport barely in time to let my wife out at the curb to check our luggage before I went to park the car. It was very close. By the time we got through security, we were minutes away from missing our flight.

The three-hour layover in Chicago wasn't as bad as we anticipated, and we subsequently arrived in Boston a little early. We waited patiently for our suitcases to get off the plane, but it took forever and we then hurriedly made our way to the car rental place. We were finally off on our big adventure.

I got the paperwork completed at the car rental place and was told to present the paperwork to the man outside and he'd show me my car. Well, the car he showed me wasn't the car I asked for when I made the reservation. It certainly wasn't one I wanted to drive. We discussed it, and he said he'd call and ask if they could bring up something else. He finally said, "What about that one?" I'll let you have it for the same rate. Perfect.

Initially, at the attendant's request, I looked around the car to see if there were any dents or nicks in the paint. Finding none, I went to the back of the car to load the luggage. I then realized I didn't have the luggage. I turned to my wife and asked, "Have you already loaded our luggage?" She responded, "What are you talking about? I don't have the luggage."

Out of sight, out of mind. I had left our suitcase in the car rental office. Finally we were set. My wife set the GPS, and we were off.

I had looked at a map and knew we were traveling I-93 into New Hampshire and Vermont. About fifteen minutes into the trip, the voice on the GPS was instructing me to turn right. I was already on I-93. I didn't need to turn right. I passed the exit, and there was this irritating voice, "Take the next right and turn around." Every exit I passed after that, same thing: "Take the next right and turn around."

We were about twenty-five miles into New Hampshire and the sound from the GPS was insufferable. "Can you turn that thing off?" my wife asked. There was something about the way she asked the question that I knew the answer was non-negotiable. I responded that we'd make it fine without the GPS. I knew we'd never make it to our destination in Quebec City, but that was tomorrow's problem. For today, we finally experienced peace and quiet in the car.

We were making good time. We were actually going to get to our hotel in Manchester sooner than I anticipated. We had plans to meet my cousin and his wife who live in New Hampshire for dinner. We were going to arrive early and I anticipated a very pleasant evening.

Out of nowhere, I said to my wife, "I'm glad I asked if you had loaded our luggage in the car. Otherwise, we wouldn't have known we didn't have it until we arrived in Manchester. That would not have been good."

My wife then said to me, "Did you get my makeup bag?"

"What makeup bag?" I replied.

"The one we checked at the airport because I couldn't carry it on the plane. Don't you remember?"

"I do now."

She must have read my mind. I was thinking, "You are a natural beauty. You really don't need makeup. We are not going back to Boston!"

Now the voice telling me to "take the next right turn and turn around" was even more insistent than the voice on the GPS. This was a "no win" situation.

We were both a little frustrated with one another by then, and we drove for several miles in complete silence. She then made the statement, "This road trip was a mistake. We shouldn't have planned to do this."

Hearing her words was like pushing the "reset button" on my attitude. I immediately regained my excitement related to the trip and said, "Lighten up! This is going to be a fun trip. We are on a big adventure, and this experience will make a great story."

The only downside is that we had dinner with my cousin a lot later than we had planned, but it was a great trip.

We reset the GPS when we got back to Boston, and it worked flawlessly for the remainder of the trip. Our experience highlights that GPS systems are very helpful when they work correctly.

In his book entitled *The Principle of the Path*, Andy Stanley states, "My observation (and experience for that matter) indicates that humans have a propensity for choosing paths that do not lead in the direction they want to go. For much of our decision-making, we lean hard into our intention and pay very little attention to the direction of the path we've chosen. I see it all the time, even with very smart people."

Stanley goes on to write,

> If you've ever gotten lost while driving (and who hasn't), you know that if you backtrack far enough, you can usually get your bearings and be on your way. Worst case, you've wasted a few minutes or hours. But when you get lost in life, you can't backtrack. When you get lost in life, you don't waste minutes or hours. You can waste an entire season of your life. Choosing the wrong path in life will cost you precious years. Nobody wants to do that.

- Nobody wants to wake up in his fifties and wish he had taken a different path in his thirties.

- Nobody wants to arrive at the end of a marriage and wish she had taken a different path during her dating years. Think about it. You only get to be twenty once.

- You get one senior year.

- You get one first marriage.

The only GPS system that is flawless is the one that addresses the spiritual dimensions of our life. "Trust in the Lord with all your heart and lean not on your own understanding; in all your ways submit to him, and he will make your paths straight" (Proverbs 3:5–6).

It seems so simple, but the correlation between the ongoing recognition of our need to trust God with our lives and our purposeful intent to allow him to direct our paths yields a sense of connectivity and a passion for living that is unparalleled. When we get to the place that ours is a "trust walk," we ultimately discover that it is more than enough.

THE LINK BETWEEN ANGER
AND FORGIVENESS

WHEN WE MOVED back to the Austin area, I found that traffic was very difficult to negotiate. Consequently, I leave for work by 6:00 a.m. every workday morning. I wouldn't describe myself as a morning person. In a perfect world, I'd still be asleep at 6:00 a.m. every morning. It gets down to picking your battles. I much prefer to be moving in a flow of traffic at 6:00 a.m. than sitting in stop-and-go traffic at 7:00 a.m. Consequently, I choose to get an early start.

Interestingly, some time ago, I made the discovery that Friday mornings seem different. Maybe it has something to do with the upcoming weekend, but I begin Friday mornings with a little more energy and enthusiasm than on the other days of the week.

A recent Friday morning seemed like a double blessing. When I walked out the door of my home, I noticed evidence that it had rained during the night. Nothing would quench my spirits now; in a few hours, I'd be into the weekend, and I didn't even have to bother with watering the lawn.

Being a little ahead of schedule, I decided to stop by the convenience store and purchase a cup of coffee. I chatted briefly with the clerk, wished her a good day, and eagerly walked out of the store to resume my commute to work.

It took me about three seconds to process that someone had parked their pickup truck directly behind my car. They had backed up next to the ice storage bin and had gone inside the store. It was probably the longest, reddest, tallest Ford pickup I'd ever seen. The heavy-duty guard on the front of the pickup even made it look more imposing. I had to walk around it to even find my car.

Unfortunately, I was hemmed in until the truck moved. There was a curb in front of me and a car parked on either side me. It was clear that I was going nowhere until the driver of the pickup returned.

It was only a little thing, but it was interfering with my Friday morning routine. I counseled myself to stay calm, drink my coffee, and enjoy the extra moments to relax. It was probably only three or four minutes, but it seemed like an eternity before the driver returned.

As he approached, I started my car. I watched in my rearview mirror as he tossed four bags of ice into the back of his truck. Before I had time to fully process what was happening, he turned and disappeared back into the store.

It may not have been my first thought, but "how inconsiderate" came to mind. Again, I found myself carrying on a dialogue with myself to calm down and patiently wait. In reality, it was only a couple of minutes before the driver returned. I saw him in my rearview mirror and anticipating his move, went ahead and put my vehicle in reverse.

I was more than a little agitated when I discovered that instead of getting inside his vehicle, he climbed into the back of the pickup. As he began pouring the bags of ice into an ice chest, I stepped out of my car thinking the reality of my presence would jolt his awareness of the need to move his vehicle. No such luck! He ignored my presence and continued with the task at hand.

I inventoried my thought process to find the right words to articulate. I wanted to say, "Hey, buddy, I'd appreciate it if you'd extend me the common courtesy of moving your truck so I can get out." However, there was something about his demeanor that led me to believe he would be resistive to social skills training. In addition, he was about twice my size. I opted to get back into my car and wait.

Later in the day, reflecting back on the experience, the thing that puzzled me was the amount of road rage I had experienced, and I wasn't even out of the parking lot. Worse yet, my feelings of exhilaration related to Friday evaporated in the midst of frustration focused on the driver of a red pickup truck.

In attempting to learn from the experience, it dawned on me that the frustration that stole the energy and enthusiasm from a Friday morning experience had something to do with misplaced priorities. From a social work perspective, I could argue that I had deferred too much responsibility for the outcome of my day to a stranger in a red pickup truck. It was simply another case of picking one's battles. This one wasn't worth the emotional energy. But what if the circumstances had been different?

A few years back, I recall experiencing an inordinate amount of stress over a several week period related to an ongoing situation at work. I have to acknowledge some ownership regarding the threshold of stress and anxiety I was experiencing. Part of the issue related to my inability to understand that if you expect irrational people to behave rationally and respectfully, you will always be disappointed. In addition, that inability really throws a question mark on whether all the parties involved had joined the ranks of the irrational.

In expressing my frustrations to my daughter, she asked a thought-provoking question. She asked, "Dad, what do you think God is trying to teach you in all of this?" My response was immediate, "Thou shalt not kill."

Don't you just hate it when your kids preach to you? Actually, the question made me very proud to be her dad. But for the moment, I didn't have time to figure out what God was trying to teach me; I was just trying to survive and orchestrate some level of civility in my world.

On occasion, my wife gets frustrated with me when I emotionally bring work home with me. It negates the opportunity for balance in my life. It is kind of like the joke where a would-be-robber pulls a gun on his victim and says, "Quick, give me your money or it's your life."

The victim responds, "I am a social worker. I have no money and I have no life."

During this stressful period in my life, my wife complained that I was spending every waking moment obsessed with work. In addition, she pointed out that she wasn't hearing me say, "I love my job."

The question my daughter had asked was a great question. "What was God trying to teach me?" Whatever it was, it was painfully obvious that I was a very slow learner.

At some point in the midst of a high-stress situation, I initiated a meeting with the founder of an organization with whom we were attempting to work. The founder in turn invited a board member to join us for the meeting. The board member was the pastor of the church the founder attended. I had not met him before.

There are some people you meet, and intuitively, you discern you'd like to get to know them better. That is not what my spirit was saying to me about this guy. Arrogant, self-righteous, controlling, vindictive, and self-centered were thoughts that came to mind in the course of our three-hour conversation. (Okay, I know what you're thinking. What happened to the biblical mandate not to be judgmental? I obviously erred.) I generally attempt to give people the benefit of the doubt, but I wasn't picking up on much that I valued.

Maybe I just don't like professional "preachers." I didn't sense much kindness…actually, I didn't sense any kindness. I have put the people that I work with on notice that if I ever come across as arrogant, self-righteous, controlling, vindictive, and self-centered, they have my permission to shoot me. It would restore some level of peace to the world and would radically enhance the work environment.

In the course of our conversation, the pastor said, "You know we don't just let anyone attend our church. We have folks who come, and if we discern they are not a fit for people we want in our church family, we ask them not to come back."

Before my conversation with him ended, he gave me a couple of directives that contradicted the written agreement that we had in place with their organization. I asked, "Are you making this request on behalf of your board?"

He said, "Yes."

The following morning, I simply confirmed back to him in writing the request he had made of me and affirmed that I would comply with his request. I sent a copy of the e-mail communication to him with a copy to the chairman of the board.

His response was to subsequently send me an e-mail denying that he had made the request. He also respectfully requested that I never contact him again. I think it was his reference to the enemy using my misperception of what had been shared to create problems that really set me off.

My initial response was to "throw up." Actually that's not true. I telephoned my boss. I am sure he had no difficulty ascertaining that I was on the verge of being out of control. He told me to calm down and work on my sermon for Sunday.

That sounded strangely close to my daughter's question, "Dad, what do you think God is trying to teach you in this?"

My immediate response was, "Then I'd better focus on forgiveness, because right now turning the other cheek is not how I'm feeling." My boss laughed and told me to have a good weekend.

At times I'm convinced that life is a lot more complicated than God intended. Have you ever stopped to consider how simple our lives could be if we relied on the leadership of the Holy Spirit to guide our relationships and serve as the baseline for every decision we make?

Several years ago, I was out of town for a week and returned to work the following Monday. When I returned, I made the discovery that an employee who worked under my supervision had made some fairly serious false allegations against me. While I was both alarmed and puzzled by the allegations, I knew they were untrue and totally without merit. It was with little effort that the truth surfaced, and I was totally vindicated.

Despite the subsequent outcome and my awareness from the onset that there was no basis for the allegations, the challenge I subsequently faced was "How do I follow the teachings of Christ related to forgiveness and relationship building?" Once the dust was settled and all was well in my world, I still had the ongoing responsibility of relating to the employee who had made the false allegations.

Theory and practice can be worlds apart in trying to implement the command of Christ when he said, "Do not resist an evildoer. But if anyone strikes you on the right cheek, turn the other also, and if anyone wants to sue you and take your coat, give your cloak as well, and if anyone forces you to go one mile, go also the second mile" (Matthew 5:39–41).

I wish I could tell you that the first thing that came to mind when I learned that a complaint had been made was the scripture that says, "Blessed are you when people revile you and persecute you and utter all kinds of evil against you falsely on my account. Rejoice and be glad, for your reward is great in heaven, for in the same way they persecuted the prophets who were before you" (Matthew 5:11–12).

Instead I found myself praying something close to the Serenity Prayer: "God grant me the serenity to accept the things I cannot change; courage to change the things I can; and the wisdom to know the difference."

Life is filled with challenges and opportunities. Isn't it our calling to glorify God in our response to what life brings our way? When forgiveness is needed, isn't it our privilege and responsibility to provide it?

I wish I could honestly tell you that all of my issues regarding forgiveness revolved around my responding to his calling on my life. Sadly, that is only one side of the story. There are many times that I have erred and need to be the recipient of someone else's forgiveness.

About six or seven years ago, a really close friend graciously orchestrated an opportunity for me to work with his company. The job offer was an incredible privilege, and I was humbled that the head of his agency was open to extending me an opportunity for employment. Truthfully, the new company could not have been more conciliatory. They had a leadership team that I highly respected. In addition, they responded positively to every need I raised as we discussed the employment opportunity.

When my current employer learned that I was in final negotiations with another company that was offering me an executive leadership position, they moved immediately to offer me the dream job of a lifetime. It took little thought on my part. I accepted.

As is often the case in life, sometimes good news is also the catalyst for bad news. I had to tell the other company that I was declining their offer. That was a tough task because they had been so patient and conciliatory.

My long-term friend did not take the news of my declining the job from his agency well. I naively assumed he'd see that I had made the best of a difficult decision. I was wrong.

I asked that he give me a call. He didn't call. I called him and left phone messages. He didn't call. I called again the following week, and he returned my call, but the conversation was very superficial.

I asked, "When are you going to be in town next? I'd like to meet you for dinner and talk."

He was honest and forthright in his response, "That's not going to happen. You don't get it, do you? I am really...." (Well, angry is what he meant.)

I got the message. I countered with something like "We've been friends for over thirty years. I'd really like to get this worked out." His response was simply, "Well, if that's how you treat a friend...."

I found the conversation very disturbing. "If that's how you treat a friend..." jolted me out of my comfort level and was the impetus for much soul-searching. Truthfully, I didn't like what I discovered. I was a real jerk!

I spent thoughtful hours beyond my "self-absorbed" comfort level and was able to process for the first time the only way my friend could have interpreted my declining the role with his agency.

I was finally at a place where I could understand the basis of my friend's anger and the feeling of betrayal he no doubt experienced related to my decision. The offer for employment had been in the making since I had made that request of him a number of years before. Truthfully, the initial request was reenforced repeatedly across the years with my continuing requests.

In response to my perceived need for something different, my friend had waited until the timing and circumstances were such that my need and his agency's need was a compatible match.

He selflessly had extended me an opportunity to join his agency as a respected peer and equal. In doing so, he carved out a portion of "who he was" and sacrificially extended that to me through the gift of friendship. It was a gift that carried with it the values and commitment that represented his agency. It was undefiled and perfect. He was handing me a "pearl of great price."

Consequently, my decision to decline the offer to share in his life's work could be construed in no other way than one of rejection.

Fortunately, my friend has the ability to offer the gift of for-giveness. Today, we continue to be good friends. He responds to God's call on his life and my life is greatly enriched by his friendship.

Lewis B. Smedes expresses it this way, "Forgiveness is God's invention for coming to terms with a world in which people are unfair to each other and hurt each other deeply. He began by forgiving us. And he invites us to forgive each other." When we can do that, it is more than enough.

THE FAMILY PET

My wife decided to name him Barnabas. He had been presented to her as a Christmas gift from our daughter. He was an eight-week-old Yorkie.

Eight months earlier, our previous dog had died. We were both pretty attached to that Yorkie. Due to work responsibilities, I traveled frequently and my wife found our dog, Brittany, to be an amiable companion. We jokingly said the dog had an IQ of 180 and spoke five languages. She was an effective communicator and fit the description of the perfect pet.

From my vantage point, it was an easy decision. There would be no more pets! We didn't need to assume responsibility for the care of anything. It was nice not having to rush home after work to attend to the needs of an animal.

I was even a little disturbed when my wife insisted we put goldfish in our outdoor pond. Didn't they need to be fed on a daily basis?

Never ever in a hundred years would I have anticipated we'd get another dog. It was not even open for debate. But there he was, in my daughter's arms as she made her way across the room toward her mother. My daughter Andrea had a smile on her face as big as Texas. In fact, so did my wife. "Mom, you're going to love your present. Isn't he precious? What are you going to name him?"

I stood by almost speechless as I processed this moving drama from across the room. The only word that came to mind was trouble. "She's going to name him Trouble," I said. "It's a perfect name for any dog."

My daughter gave me one of those "Oh, Dad, go away" looks. It was clear that this was an interaction reserved only for her mother.

Kevin, my daughter's fiancée, observed the interaction without saying a word. I subsequently cornered him and inquisitively asked, "How did you allow this to happen?" Actually, I may have grabbed him by both shoulders to get his attention. I wanted him to know that my comments about the dog were not, tongue in cheek. I really did not want another dog.

Cute is not the first word that came to mind as I realized I didn't even get a vote in the matter. Like it or not, Barnabas had come to stay.

I have never considered myself as having attachment issues, but it took me about six weeks to begin to warm toward Barnabas. By then, I had observed there were times that he was personable and cute. His dark eyes communicated a world of playfulness and energy. I had even begun to think he had the potential to become the highly regarded family pet.

One thing was for certain, after six weeks, it was abundantly clear that my wife was not going to come to her senses and decide to find a home for Barnabas with another family somewhere else. Barnabas was with us to stay.

That is not to say my earlier announcement was incorrect. The dog represents trouble and lots of it. Tending to his needs on a daily basis can be tiring and a little overwhelming. It seems like every step we took in the direction of getting him trained was followed by two steps backward.

Barnabas has now been with us for eleven years. I keep telling myself he still has potential, but he is not always respectful of the limits or boundaries I think he should keep. I've even asked myself, "What am I supposed to learn from this experience?"

Sometimes, when I watch him playing in the front yard, I wonder how often God is tempted to throw up his hands in frustration with the way I keep making the same mistakes and failing to be open to his leadership and direction. There are times that I am very much like Barnabas. I do "dog things" instead of "divine things."

God has demonstrated over and over again that he is a loving master. Isn't it true that he gently redirects and patiently loves us despite our failure and shortcomings? Perhaps from his perspective, he sees us as having potential. We are created in his image and designed to have fellowship with him. We are created to be his constant companions. Hopefully at some point, we will demonstrate actual progress rather than raw potential.

My wife is pretty protective of Barnabas. Somehow, whenever he does something wrong, she sees some correlation to my failure to be responsible. I haven't figured that out yet.

One Saturday morning, I opted to do yard work. It was about noon, and I was almost finished for the day. Unfortunately, I inadvertently left the gate open. It only took a split-second, but Barnabas darted out of the yard like he'd been freed from prison and took off running as fast as he could. (Every time something like that happens, my wife thinks it is my fault. From her perspective, responsible people don't leave the gate open.)

Although I knew it was futile, I started calling his name followed by "treat." Knowing my death was imminent if I didn't recover the dog, I went inside and got the dog's jar of treats and started out in pursuit. I was hopeful that none of our neighbors could hear me, but I was repeatedly calling out, "Barnabas, treat."

They say the most important sound in the universe is the sound of your name. I was recently half paying attention on a conference call and tuned into the conversation when I heard the question, "Don, what do you think?" Let me tell you, you can articulate the name "Barnabas" until you are out of breath; it doesn't make a difference. He may or may not respond.

The temperature was over one hundred degrees. I looked for Barnabas for over an hour. I was sweaty, hot, miserable, and mad. I didn't have time for this. I even found myself asking, "God, what am I supposed to learn from this?" I didn't get an answer. I was still hot. I was sweaty, thirsty, and frustrated.

At some level, I was concerned for Barnabas's safety. I had walked over a number of acres, and he was nowhere in sight. He is a very small dog, and there are coyotes in the area. I didn't want him to become lunch for a coyote or to make his way to the road where he could easily have hitched a ride with a passerby who wanted a cute dog.

If I'm going to be totally honest, I also didn't want to have to deal with a lecture from my wife about being irresponsible and not paying attention. She seldom begins by saying, "If I've told you once, I've told you a thousand times…," but she could have chosen to go there. We've certainly had this same conversation several times.

Things don't have to be as difficult as Barnabas chooses to make them. I simply want him to come to me when I call his name. Could it be that God wants the same thing with me? He calls my name and I'm so caught up with whatever activity I'm involved in that I fail to hear his call. In many respects, I am very much like Barnabas.

I was hot, miserable, frustrated, dehydrated, and angry. The dog was nowhere to be found. Still I was resolved to find him before returning home. I was startled by the sound of my cell phone ringing. It was my wife. She called to let me know that Barnabas had returned.

That proved to be an insightful lesson for me. From that day on, anytime Barnabas has managed to escape from the yard, it has been his full responsibility to make his way back home. I have chosen not to go looking for him.

One Friday evening, my wife and I had an out-of-town work obligation. Consequently, the responsibility fell on me to transport Barnabas to the kennel for boarding on Friday morning.

By the time I got to the kennel, I was literally covered with dog hair. My sports coat was covered. My shirt was covered. My slacks were covered. I looked like John the Baptist had picked out my clothing for the day. I was less than pleased.

The folks at the kennel seemed glad to see Barnabas. And of course, I was glad to see them too. Surprisingly, they had a lot of questions for me:

- Did I want to have Barnabas bathed while he was there? I responded, "No, my wife gave him a bath last night."

- Did I want them to arrange extra "playtime" for Barnabas? It was another easy answer, "No." I fought back the urge to say I want him to have a safe place to eat and sleep. This is intended to be a "no frills" kind of experience.

- Did I want them to take Barnabas on a nature walk? (I have never been around folks who do drugs, but I was beginning to wonder what they had been smoking.) Nature walk? The kennel is located thirty feet off the highway. You can stand on the sidewalk and imagine you're in the middle of a freeway. It was hardly a place of serenity. "Nature walk?" I don't think so.

- Would I like for them to provide Barnabas a "pupsicle" for a snack in the middle of the afternoon? "No, he doesn't generally eat pupsicles." (I wanted to say, "Only if the 'ice cream man' comes by in a van that plays music.")

The lady asking the questions looked at me with a look of disdain and admonishingly stated, "I bet you don't want him to have a massage either." I responded, "Probably not. I don't even treat myself in that regard, but thanks for asking."

Finally the questions were over. Barnabas was safely entrusted to someone else's care, and I was on my way to work, dog hair and all.

I was hardly back in the midst of traffic before I was feeling guilty. I started wondering, "What is wrong with me? My wife would have said yes and arranged for Barnabas to participate in at least half of the amenities they offered." I then wondered, "Am I too cheap to provide for the dog's best interest?" Worse yet, "Would the kennel be making a referral to the humane society suggesting I'm not fit to care for a dog?"

There are days I wonder if I have an attachment disorder when it comes to pets. It isn't that I have absolutely no interest in animals, but I don't personally have a need to be a full-time pet owner. I would much prefer animals be someone else's responsibility.

My daughter and son-in-law have two labs. They bring them over often. My daughter has an aversion to leaving the dogs alone at home if they can be with them. She and my son-in-law have absolutely no attachment issues related to their pets. They want to be with them. Consequently, whenever they come to visit, the dogs come with them.

Samson and Colby, the two dogs, either love me or they are both passive aggressive. Every time they come through the door, they make a beeline to me. The attention they devote would make anyone feel good. Consequently, I've figured out that the attention is probably one of the reasons pet owners choose to have labs. I guess it is a trade-off for the excessive amount of hair they shed and their innate ability to slobber or drool after they've had a drink of water.

Labs sit at your feet. When you stand to move to another room, they move with you. They then reposition themselves to again sit at your feet. One gets the sense that you must represent some kind of royalty from the level of attention the dogs shower on you.

I will be the first to admit that my tendency toward being obsessive-compulsive probably negates my ability to be perfectly comfortable with the level of disarray animals are capable of producing. I want everything neat, proper, and in its place. That doesn't always happen with animals.

There is a life lesson in that observation. We, too, are the creation of a God who intended more for our existence than we have proven capable of fulfilling. We routinely not only make a mess of our environment, we also at times make a mess of our lives. We have repeatedly "fallen short of the glory of God." Despite the mess, God is firmly committed to embracing us with his unconditional love. We don't have to get it right to be loved by God. That reality gives us the understanding that his love is more than enough.

FAMILY TREASURE

I NEVER THOUGHT about my dad being a collector. He lived very simply and would never avail himself to an inordinate need for things. He was without doubt the most unpretentious person I've ever known. Consequently, I was surprised after his death to make the discovery that my dad kept a lot of stuff for "just in case" emergencies. My best guess is that propensity was a hold over from the depression years.

- Now that he was gone, what was I supposed to do with a five-gallon bucket of nuts and bolts? I couldn't imagine finding what you might need even if you needed something. The amount of time it would take to sort through a bucket that size seemed counterproductive to me. Fortunately, I found someone who thought they might find a use for them. I gladly gave them away.

- Dad had five or six pipe wrenches. In scrambling to bring closure to his home, I gave most of them away to other people. I opted to keep a couple of the pipe wrenches knowing full well that I would never use them. To my knowledge, Dad didn't use them either. Perhaps there is something in my DNA that allows keeping things for "just in case" you need them.

- There was a set of metal ramps Dad used to elevate the front of his car when he changed the oil. My dad was eighty-one years old when he moved. I remember at the time suggesting that he would not need the ramps after the move. It was my belief that at his age, he didn't need to be crawling under a car to change the oil. Interestingly, he insisted the ramps not be excluded from the move.

- I had the passing thought that perhaps it was pay-back time. How many times across the years did I ask my dad for advice and then choose to do what I wanted despite his wise counsel to do it differently? It was more times than I'd like to remember.

- Dad also had two sets of chains. I have absolutely no idea when or why he acquired them. I was equally insistent that he leave the chains behind. We didn't need to bother moving them. Again, before the move was completed, we opted to do it Dad's way. "You never know when you'll need to pull someone out of a ditch" was his way of justifying the need to keep the chains.

- After Dad's death, I took delight in insisting that my younger brother take Dad's military overcoat from WWII. After all, Dad had kept the coat for over sixty years. It didn't seem right to throw it away. I was subsequently in for a surprise when I later discovered Dad's military uniform in the closet. If the logic I used with my brother was sound, perhaps I was now obligated to have the ominous task of storing the uniform for the remainder of my days.

I was in Houston a short time later and wandered through Barnes and Noble. Mistakenly, prior to that time, the last place

I'd ever think to look for a religious book was Barnes and Noble. I was very surprised to discover that they had a large inventory of books in the "Religious" section. Looking at the prices, I could do the math in my head. The books were less expensive there than at a traditional Christian bookstore. I connected the dots, and now I purchase all of my books from Barnes and Noble.

Surprise of surprises, I found a newly released John Ortberg book entitled *When the Game Is Over, It All Goes Back in the Box.* Even without reading the cover, I knew intuitively that it was a must-have. Subsequently, in the course of my reading, I connected the dots and thought of the daunting task of bringing closure to my parent's home.

Ortberg expressed it this way: "People go through life, get stuff, and then they die leaving all their stuff behind. What happens to it? The kids argue over it. The kids—who haven't died yet, who are really just pre-dead people—go over to their parents' house. They pick through their parent's old stuff like vultures, deciding which stuff they want to take to their houses. They say to themselves, 'Now this is my stuff.' Then they die and some new vultures come for it. People come and go. Nations go to war over stuff. Families are split apart because of stuff. Husbands and wives argue more about stuff than any other single issue."

We give priority to the accumulation of stuff and subsequently discover that finding places to store it at times poses a problem. Out of curiosity, I did a Google search related to "the self-storage industry in our country." I was surprised with the findings:

- The self-storage industry has been one of the fastest-growing sectors of commercial real estate in the United States over the last thirty-five years.

- There are approximately 49,940 "primary" self storage facilities in the United States as of year end 2011. (With 85 percent of approximately 58,500 self-storage facilities worldwide.)

- Total self-storage rentable space in the US is now 2.3 billion square feet. That figure represents more than seventy-eight square miles of rentable self-storage space, under roof—or an area well more than three times the size of Manhattan Island, NY.

- Gross revenues for US self-storage facilities for 2011 were approximately $22.45 billion (If you need a frame of reference, the music industry only generated $16.5 billion in 2011.)

- One in ten US households currently rent a self-storage unit.

Fortunately, conflict related to honoring my parent's wishes related to distribution of their estate was a non-issue. Never ever would we have considered anything other than an equal distribution according to their instruction. In fact, when we were attempting to vacate their home and get it ready to place on the market, we invited extended family members outside the scope of immediate family to go through their home and take anything they wanted. My parents were loved and respected by their siblings and their nieces and nephews. I couldn't think of a more appropriate way to honor my folks than sharing keepsakes, mementos, and things treasured.

The subsequent downside of packing their things and vacating their home was finding a place to store the things that others didn't take but held some level of sentimental value. We opted to store several boxes hurriedly filled with family pictures and keepsakes in our upstairs bedroom. Since the upstairs room is almost never used, it seemed like an ideal place to temporarily store things until we had the time to casually sort through them and determine what to keep and what to throw away.

Have you ever been resistive to "getting through the clutter"? Truthfully, there are times my to-do list includes chores I'd just as soon forget about and never get around to completing. Recently, my wife and I invited several extended family members to come for a weekend visit. Anticipating their arrival, my wife insisted that it was time for us to remove the clutter from the upstairs guest room. My initial reaction was to ignore her request, but I knew her determined resolve would be the catalyst that provided constant reminders until the task was completed.

Some folks would call that "nagging." Yet I couldn't be too critical because I knew she was right. Still somewhat resistive and dreading the task, I went upstairs to survey the boxes. Somehow, despite my effort, I couldn't convince myself that the stored items would be okay to leave for another day. Something needed to be done if the room was to be comfortably habitable.

Even with both of us sorting through a lifetime of photos, keepsakes, and a few pieces of correspondence my folks obviously valued and protected, the task was not quickly nor easily negotiated. Initially, it was enjoyable to view photos of family members from far away and long ago.

Whether purposefully or involuntarily, my mind drifted back across the years and relived some of the times captured in fading photographs. I would turn one picture over only to be confronted by another memory from my childhood or early adulthood. The process was filled with emotional moments as I contemplated the reality that many of the family members depicted in photographs have been separated from this side of eternity for a very long time. Despite their physical absence, the range of influence and value they continue to pour into my life through memories too precious to forget continue to resonate with freshness and purpose.

In going through my parents' keepsakes, I picked up an envelope addressed to my parents. The envelope contained a letter an aunt had written to my parents during a very painful period in our family's history. The letter was kind and comforting and obviously intended to provide encouragement and hope. From the content, I could understand why my folks chose to cherish the correspondence.

The range of emotion it evoked was pretty overpowering. As subtly as I could, I bolted from the upstairs room and rushed outside for a breather. Once I had regained my composure, I came back inside and returned to the task before us. Shortly afterward, my wife picked up another envelope, looked at the address and date stamp, and said, "Here is a letter you wrote to your parents in 1965. Do you want to read it?"

I didn't even have to think about it. The answer was simply "No."

I don't know if "we" opted to keep the letter or throw it away. I still don't want to read it, but I've wondered several times over the past few weeks what unseen treasure the envelope contained that would have justified my parents keeping it since 1965. I can only imagine that I was expressing gratitude and thanksgiving for the love, security, and nurture they provided throughout my childhood and for the encouragement and support they were continuing to provide at the threshold of my adulthood years. That would be the kind of communication that a parent would never tire of hearing. It would be a catalyst to affirm they were valued and loved. In short, they did their job as parents and they did it extremely well.

As I've pondered the possible content of the letter my parents chose as a keepsake, the thought occurred to me: What sentiments of my heart and expressions of gratitude articulated to God across the years, does God choose to remember? Does he periodically remind himself that there are some times in our relationship that I seem to understand, occasions where I'm overwhelmed by his grace and his love, and periods where the passion of my life is "to know him" and yield to his leadership? Does he cherish those brief moments of connectedness and comfort himself when my mistaken direction and lack of faithfulness obscure my walk with him?

Fortunately, Christ intercedes in our behalf. Our relationship to God is not dependent on our performance. Through his sacrifice, Christ is able to sympathize with our weaknesses and provide opportunity for us to come boldly to the throne of grace where we obtain mercy and help. That reality is more than enough.

EXTENDED FAMILY:
ONE STEP REMOVED

DURING MY CHILDHOOD years, my paternal grandparents gave priority and attention to family reunions. Once each year, they purposefully gathered with their siblings and other extended family members in some location in close proximity to their old home place and took the time to visit with family members and catch up with events over the past year.

Since the reunions generally took place 350 miles from where we lived, it was infrequent that my family attended. My dad generally had to work half a day on Saturdays. During my childhood years, it was a priority for my grandparents, but not necessarily one for my dad. Consequently, I reached adulthood without having a lot of familiarity with any of my dad's extended family. Of course we were close to his brother's family, but as far as his cousins and other extended family members, it was infrequent that our paths connected.

Although my grandparents' generation has long since gone on to be with the Lord, the tradition of an annual family reunion has continued. Sometimes in deference to my grandparent's memory, I choose to honor them by making an appearance on their behalf. It also provides me an opportunity to drive by their old home place and to visit their gravesites. The process always provides a flood of wonderful memories, and I emerge from the experience with a renewed appreciation for the impact and influence my grandparents contributed to my life.

My attempt at extended family interaction has sometimes proven interesting. About twenty years ago, my daughter who was about eleven years of age accompanied me to a reunion of my paternal grandmother's family. Unknown to me at the time, the reunion site was hosting two extended families that had some kind of connection to our family through marriage. Not everyone was actually related, but someone thought this co-mingling of two extended families was a good idea.

Shortly after arriving, someone I had never seen before commented to me, no doubt well intentioned, that I had a beautiful granddaughter. I calmly replied that she was not my granddaughter but my daughter. As a side note, I may have looked three days older than dirt at the age of forty-five, but there was no way I looked old enough to have an eleven-year-old granddaughter. How absurd! (Actually, I thought it was funny, and I added it to my memory bank as a great story to share).

About an hour later, someone else, perhaps linking my last name to that of an aunt with the same last name, asked if she was my wife. Ouch! I didn't see that one coming. My aunt was at least twenty years older than me. Surely I didn't look that old. It was strictly coincidental, but it wasn't long afterward that I came up with a legitimate reason to excuse myself and head back for home. After all, it was a six-hour drive, and I needed to get ready for church the following day.

Subsequent reunions have left me with other good stories. Connecting with my grandmother's extended family has been a positive experience.

Interestingly, I noticed that following my dad's retirement, he and my mother started giving priority to being present for the family reunions and having opportunities to interact with cousins. It was similar to the commitment demonstrated by my grandparents with their siblings. In the process of their involvement, I have learned to enjoy the brief annual interaction with members of my dad's extended family.

I recall attending a reunion about ten years ago that was a little unsettling for me. I emerged from the experience grateful for the opportunity to interact and visit with relatives that I seldom had an opportunity to see. Despite the fact that the reunion was an upbeat experience, my casual observation of the health status of many of my dad's cousins left me with a sense of foreboding. It was almost as if overnight, some family members in my father's age range had become wrought with serious health issues and life-threatening difficulties.

It dawned on me that my dad's generation has moved up a step. They now more closely represented the generation that was reflective of the most recent memories of my grandparents and their siblings.

Perhaps on an unconscious level, I, too, was resistive to the notion that I had moved up a notch. Certainly there are days that I have the sense that perhaps I have become my father. Sometimes I catch a look in the mirror and don't always see the type A, energetic and outgoing, action-oriented workaholic that was more reflective of my former years. I'd like to think I've matured and now exercise more discretion in those activities with which I choose to devote my time. Perhaps that's part of the maturing process. I can't be old enough to be my father, but I am startled to see him looking back at me in the mirror. Perhaps the same is true for you.

Truthfully, after the death of my dad and his brother, the desire to continue connecting with their extended family members that I have always had little-to-no contact with diminished to some degree. There are three or four of my dad's cousins that I've always looked up to and welcome contact with, but the majority are mostly strangers to me. Consequently, the need to carve out a six-hour trip each way on either side of a family reunion didn't make the reunion seem like a priority.

Recently, at the urging of one of my dad's cousins whom I dearly love, I decided I'd attend the reunion. Work obligations found me in Houston the day before the family reunion. It made no sense to drive back home to Austin before I headed northward. Knowing my schedule, I had hoped to coordinate my arrival at the time my younger brother would be joining me there. He would be traveling from the Tulsa area.

Unfortunately, a couple of days before the reunion, my brother was in an automobile accident that left him pretty shaken. He wasn't seriously injured, but he opted to cancel on the reunion. If it had not been for the commitment to attend that I previously made to my dad's cousin, I would have canceled as well. Because of her ongoing invitation to "please come," I found it important to keep my commitment.

I drove from Houston to Dallas on Friday evening and spent the night. Morning found me up early and awaiting the day to coordinate my schedule to arrive before noon. Until then, I hadn't even considered that I needed to bring a covered dish or two. I couldn't show up empty-handed.

As I continued to travel northward, I thought I'd stop in at a KFC and purchase a couple of buckets of chicken and some side dishes. That seemed like my only real solution.

As I was en route, I called my brother in Oklahoma and shared with him my plan for handling food. He responded, "Don't do that. Go to Walmart. They have great chicken strips. They really are very good. We buy them every year for my wife's family reunion. Everyone likes them."

There are basically two types of people in the word: those who think Walmart has everything you need and those who won't go in Walmart. Whether purposeful or otherwise, I have a tendency to fall in the latter group. I decided, based on my brother's recommendation, to go with his plan.

I took out my iPhone and searched for Walmart when I got to the next town. It wasn't difficult to find. I made my way to the food court and ordered a sizeable amount of chicken strips. The person who waited on me said, "We don't have the amount you need already prepared. Could you give us thirty minutes?" I hadn't planned on taking thirty minutes out of my day, but I said, "Sure."

I took the time to look around Walmart. Actually, I was favorably impressed with the store. The favorable impression changed when I went back thirty minutes later to pick up the chicken and side orders. The person I had placed the order with reportedly had gone on break. The employee I was now talking with didn't know anything about my order, but it was not prepared.

What do you do? The only thing I could think to do was rearticulate what I wanted. Again, I was asked to wait while the order was prepared. Eventually, I got my order. I also silently made the resolve that this was my last trip to Walmart.

When I arrived at the family reunion, I was surprised by the number of cars parked around the building. Cars were everywhere. When I walked into the room, I was startled. Initially, I didn't see anyone that I knew. The introvert who lives inside me wanted to run away. I calmed him down and starting looking for folks I knew.

In short order, I found family members that I knew and felt a little more comfortable. They seemed pleased that I had come. At some point in the next few minutes, I called my wife and told her I was mostly surrounded by people I didn't know. She put a positive spin on my plight by telling me to "make new friends." I didn't think it was funny.

There were probably a hundred people in the room and the vast majority were people I did not know. I opted to talk exclusively with the folks I knew and made no effort to accept the challenge of making new friends.

When it was time to line up for lunch, I opted to wait until others were served. As I waited at my table, I had the passing thought that I should have a mental health assessment. I had driven six hours in the car to get to the reunion, incurred the expense of a hotel room in Dallas, spent enough money at Walmart for a really good meal elsewhere, and I was now mostly surrounded by people I didn't know.

Driving back to the Austin area later that evening, I took the chance to ask God what I was supposed to learn from the experience. The response was forthcoming and almost immediate. We have a relationship with God through faith in Christ, but how well do we really know him? What does it mean to be a follower of Christ? What does it mean to live under the leadership of God?

Are there times I am no more familiar with God than I was with the majority of distant relatives whose names I didn't know and who seemingly didn't know me? Instead of building on the strengths that we share related to heritage, I opted to play the recluse and left without making new friends. Does God find me equally distant and unfriendly?

Actually, the reunion could have been more enjoyable than I allowed. I have no one to blame but myself. I am grateful for my heritage, and I am grateful for the lineage that is mine. Hopefully, next time, I'll make a better effort of connecting with folks who share the same ancestry as me. If that can happen, it will be more than enough.

'TIL DEATH DO US PART

ABOUT THIRTY-FIVE YEARS ago, one of the men who attended the same Sunday school class that I attended had an experience that immediately substantiated that he lived in denial. In addition, he was clearly out of touch with reality.

He was out tending his garden one Saturday morning when a sheriff's car pulled up in front of his house. The garden was located on property adjacent to the house. My friend walked over and asked the officer if he could help. "I'm looking for…"

The man responded, "You've found me. What can I help you with?"

He was surprised with the response, "I have some papers for you."

The officer served him with legal papers notifying him that his wife had filed for divorce. The strange thing was that his wife was inside their home. He was dumbfounded. From his perspective, they had a perfect marriage.

I share that information in the form of a disclaimer, but I think I can safely say that my wife and I have a nearly perfect marriage. The only consistent complaint she ever makes is that (and this is based solely on her perception) I don't pay attention. She says it happens all the time. Reportedly, she'll tell me something, only later to have me discover information that seems like new information.

It wasn't that long ago that she asked about the time of my doctor's appointment scheduled for later that day. I responded late afternoon. Actually the appointment was scheduled for 2:30 p.m., but my experience is such that I know that I'll wait at least an hour before I get in to see the doctor regardless of the time of the appointment. Consequently, late afternoon was about as specific as I could get.

When I got home that evening, my wife mentioned something her doctor had told her that day. I was puzzled. That morning, she had asked about my doctor's appointment but never mentioned that she, too, was going for a scheduled examination. I asked why she didn't tell me she had a doctor's appointment. She stated empathically that she told me earlier that morning when she asked about my appointment. She even highlighted the fact that her doctor is located in the same building where my doctor is located.

I guess I take some kind of satisfaction out of knowing that her biggest dissatisfaction with me is something as simple as my not paying attention. I can think of so many things far more grievous than that. I'd say that she's a lucky woman.

I probably should tell you up front that I married way above my pay group. That is not to say that our marriage has always been easy. Marriage is hard work. It is easy to fall in love. It is relatively easy to be in love. But it takes deliberate ongoing conscious effort to always choose to be loving.

When we first married, one of the techniques we used to manage conflict resolution was pretty simple. I screamed and she cried. That worked fairly well for about a year and a half. The next year and a half, she screamed and I cried. Since then, we've matured a lot and found healthier ways of resolving conflict.

After forty-six years of marriage, our periods of conflict seldom surface. Our priorities have blended, and we generally are in agreement on almost everything. I am very grateful that she's become very much like me. Actually, that is not accurate. We both have made some positive changes and now find ourselves a lot closer to being alike on the things that really matter. Our style and approach in getting it accomplished isn't always congruent, but we work well together.

Together we have crafted out a kaleidoscope of memories that add much to our sense of well-being. Throughout our journey, we have repeatedly experienced the ongoing gift of love and kindness from family and friends. Our lives have been full. In addition, my wife has proven to be an incredible helpmate, mother, grandmother, friend, encourager, and companion. I could long for nothing more.

Sometimes I initiate a discussion just for the joy of getting her response. On a recent Saturday morning, we were headed different directions. My wife had a beauty shop appointment, and I was going to work. As I was leaving, I turned to her and said, "Don't forget, you are the only you God made."

She looked at me like I was nuts and replied, "Aren't you glad?"

With the diplomacy of a statesman, I responded, "Our world would be better if there were more people like you, but truthfully, one of you is quite enough for me." With that affirmation of kindness, I walked out the door. (Okay, I guess it is a judgment call if it was an affirmation of kindness, "Our world would be better if there were more people like you"—that is kind. Perhaps the jury is still out on "one of you is quite enough for me.")

Like my friend who was working in his garden, I'd say we have a nearly perfect marriage. In a perfect world, I could make a suggestion or two of things that she could do differently, but I am managing fine with the status quo.

I don't know about you, but I sometimes get a little frustrated when the conversation begins with "You need to…"

Off and on over several months, my wife gently nudged me to purchase an external hard drive for my computer. Of course, her intentions are always well-intended, but her obsessive-compulsive nature of taking care of business in an orderly and timely fashion can at times be a little irritating. That is particularly true when her priorities are incongruent with mine and the nudging begins with "You need to…"

It is fairly obvious to people who know both of us that we are as different as night and day. My general approach to life is more laidback than hers. I like to do things on the spur of the moment. I call it living impromptu. She, on the other hand, is a planner. Her organizational skills and compulsivity to get it done early defies explanation. I maintain if it wasn't for the last minute, a lot of things would never get done.

Of course, I can't argue with the fact that her logic is sound. If my computer crashed and I lost everything I've written over the past six years, I'd be distraught. It certainly would cause a major delay in the book I've promised to pull together for my children and grandchildren.

It also doesn't help my attitude when my wife suggests that I need to get to work on the book now because, at my age, I may not have much time left. (Actually, she has never mentioned my age or the amount of time I have left, but she has been like the inopportune widow in the parable that Jesus told regarding the widow's request for justice. The judge finally granted her request simply to keep her from coming back to his courtroom.)

Subsequently, we were purchasing printer cartridges for each of our computers and she said to me, "You need to pick up an external hard drive for your computer while we are here."

I finally gave in. I hauled the thing home and sat it in the corner of my office. The directions on the box didn't seem that clear to me. I decided I'd wait until someone more knowledgeable about computers came by so I could ask for assistance.

The next weekend, with the help of my son-in-law, I finally connected the device to my computer. I was surprised when I took it out of the box. It was not nearly as large or invasive as I thought it would be. It was Styrofoam, not the device, that filled most of the box. I was glad. I didn't want anything large or bulky on my desk.

When we hooked it up, it became obvious immediately that it was going to take forever to download the programs that needed to be installed in order for the backup device to work. I didn't understand any of it, but I suggested to my son-in-law that he didn't need to stay until everything was downloaded. I could manage from here.

It proved to be a very slow day for the Internet. My wife and I opted to drive into town before the download was completed. When we returned, I couldn't ascertain anything related to the status of the download. I was a little frustrated, but I shrugged it off. What was one more day? As it turned out, I subsequently learned the downloads failed.

You guessed it. The ensuing rainstorm the following morning was the catalyst that fried my computer. How many times do you have to plug and unplug a computer before you finally realize the computer isn't working? I won't tell you how many times I tried, but I finally became convinced it was not coming back on. I hate it when my wife is right! I should have taken care of the situation months earlier.

It may have taken great resolve on her part to refrain from saying those words, but she never suggested once that if I had followed her wise counsel, the outcome would have been different. What she did express was empathy and understanding.

One of the ongoing strengths that she displays is encouragement. She is my greatest cheerleader. She never expresses doubt that I have the skill and ability "to make the team" regardless of the venue under discussion. Wow! I told you I married well.

Expressing that "I married well" is not synonymous with the notion that "we are always in agreement." While our home was still under construction, we noticed a couple of barn swallows swooping through and around the covered porch on the back of the house.

When I subsequently discovered they were starting a nest, my initial reaction was to disrupt the building of the nest. After all, I didn't want birds sharing space with me on the back porch. My wife, on the other hand, thought offering a sanctuary for a couple of birds seemed inconsequential. Besides that, she thought they were pretty. Her vote was clearly to leave the birds alone and allow them to build their nest wherever they saw fit.

The experience proved to be a crash course in assisting us in remembering why we don't have a parakeet. We don't want to be bothered by the mess. After all, someone has to clean the birdcage. Sharing one's porch and patio area with a family of birds is tantamount to having feathered friends that don't pick up after themselves. It's a lot of trouble if you want to maintain the area for your use as well.

Consequently, the following year, my wife's attitude was significantly different. (I am resisting the notion of suggesting that she is, at times, a slow learner.) When she spotted two swallows sitting on the ledge that offered sanctuary to the family of feathered friends the year before, her first reaction was not a warm welcome. It came close to a mandate, "We've got to do something!"

She then began a litany of "home remedies" she'd been told that would preclude the desirability of birds nesting on our home. According to her, we had two options. We could place rubber snakes around the ledges or we could find an artificial owl that would frighten the birds away.

Since rubber snakes hold the potential of also frightening me away, I opted to steer her toward the artificial owl section of the hardware store. The owl certainly wasn't going to add to the aesthetic value of our patio area, not to mention it cost four times what I thought it was worth. In the final analysis, the only debate was whether to purchase one owl or two. Fortunately, my vote prevailed, and we only bought one.

The long and short of it, the artificial owl didn't work. It was almost like a calling card for swallows. The numbers that subsequently appeared reminds me of a sequel to Alfred Hitchcock's movie *The Birds*. Swallows appeared out of everywhere. They certainly had no aversion to the artificial owl strategically placed on the patio and, almost as an act of defiance, flew directly over my head.

My wife no longer thinks of swallows as looking pretty. Now when she sees them, she conjures up a visual image of the mess they subsequently leave behind. They no longer appear nearly as attractive as her initial first impression.

We had a similar disagreement when it came to purchasing a new area rug for our living area. Since we have a dog that is not always respectful of rugs, I was insistent that we not purchase an expensive rug. We have an expensive rug in our dining room, and I keep the room barricaded to ensure the integrity of the rug. I didn't want to have the same level of stress associated with an area rug in an open area of our home.

I suggested that we shop for a rug at a large store that specialized in rugs. Once arriving, I was surprised to learn that my wife thought we should purchase a rug very different from any rug we've ever owned. She thought it would be nice to select something very modern and contemporary. "It would be good for a change" is the way she expressed it. I was horrified.

Did I mention that our home and furnishings are not modern and contemporary? We historically have chosen to furnish and decorate our homes in a very traditional style. We also have a lot of artwork in our living area, and it is primarily works by G. Harvey. The thought of adding contemporary and modern to the look that currently prevails didn't make sense to me.

The first rug she selected closely resembled a work of art by Jackson Pollock. It was a myriad of lots of different colors and patterns. I remember thinking, "I don't know this woman. Who is she? What is she thinking?"

Truthfully, if we lived in a high-rise apartment in downtown Austin with lots of glass and a totally open setting, the rug would have been great as long as the furniture coordinated with the style. Getting back to reality, we didn't live in an Austin high rise and we didn't have contemporary furniture. The new look she was suggesting didn't work for me.

I attempted to show her what I thought we needed. It wasn't even a consideration. "We've had that look before, I want something different," she countered.

I never anticipated that we would spend all afternoon looking at rugs. When we finally selected something we both agreed on, the rug was very different from what either of us initially thought we wanted. Perhaps through the process of elimination (or maybe exhaustion), we both thought we were winning and we went home with a sigh of relief related to what could have been if either of us had gone shopping alone.

Some time ago, I made a Facebook query regarding my friends. I asked for responses to the question "What is your greatest fear?" I subsequently learned two things:

- Most of my friends have no fear. They didn't make a response to my question.

- Almost without fail, everyone who responded stated their greatest fear was that their husband or wife would precede them in death.

I was taken back by the responses. The expressed fear that one's spouse would precede them in death seemed surreal. The fear seemed developmentally inappropriate to me. My peer group surely has not reached the age that such fear would be commonplace, has it?

In reflecting back on the answers, I almost had a panic attack thinking of the possibility. If my wife preceded me in death, I wouldn't even be able to drive without her. Who would tell me to slow down, change lanes, turn here, etc.?

That is only the beginning of the difficulties that would entail. I agree with God, "It is not good for man to be alone" (Genesis 2:18). I am grateful for the privilege of sharing life with a help-mate. I like the way the New English Bible states it, "I will provide a partner for him." That gift has been more than enough.

THE FRUIT DOESN'T FALL
FAR FROM THE TREE

I PROCESSED IT as a tongue-in-cheek e-mail sent to me by a friend. Knowing my friend's political candor, it was intended to be more humorous than thought-provoking. The article was cleverly presented and used oil company logos throughout the text. Of course, the thrust of the article suggested that oil was the primary reason for the war with Iraq. As far as junk e-mail goes, I thought it qualified for at least an honorable mention.

Never thinking for a moment that others would find the e-mail offensive or politically insensitive, I forwarded it to my son. It was clear from his response that he failed to see the same humor that I had gleaned. In short order, he responded by writing, "What liberal sent this to you? How about disarming an evil regime of weapons of mass destruction? Better yet, how about ending thirty years of rape, torture, and murder? The next time someone tells you that the war is all about oil, ask them if they walked to work that day."

Ouch! I'd never have forwarded the e-mail to my son if I'd thought for a minute he would fail to see the humor in it. On the other hand, perhaps his response was also "tongue in cheek." In sharing his response with a co-worker, she made some comment about the "fruit not falling too far from the tree."

I was reluctant to ask for clarification. Did she think it was clever and timely? Or was she implying that at times, I, too, am fairly opinionated? If that is what she meant, it would carry a second ouch with it.

One of the ongoing joys of my life relates to my relationship with my children and their families. Ours is a close-knit clan, and the value we give toward maintaining a sense of connectedness is both refreshing and atypical of many families that I know. My daughter has communicated (tongue-in-cheek, I hope) to her brother that she has maintained primary responsibility for our oversight and supervision for the past ten years. She expressed her willingness to sign on for ten more years, but after that, we are his responsibility.

Some time ago, I visited with a long-time friend who was estranged from his family. At the time of our visit, he had been separated from his wife for a couple of years. I was shocked when I learned of their separation. His wife is one of the most delightful people that I know. What was he thinking? My friend and I are the same age. Consequently, he is way too old for a midlife crisis.

My friend has three adult children. During our visit, he shared that his youngest daughter had called and wanted to visit with him. He said that prior to meeting with her, he had a lot of anxiety and fear related to what she might say. Was she going to give him an ultimatum regarding his relationship with her mother?

Instead of an ultimatum regarding her mother, she expressed the need for his involvement in orchestrating a sense of calm between her siblings. He responded that they didn't need his involvement to orchestrate peace. They were adults and were responsible for their own behavior. He stated he had already done his job and the rest was up to them.

He didn't ask for my opinion, but I felt obligated as his friend to provide a different frame of reference. I told him I could understand his position, but that I didn't agree with him. I said to him, "Sure, your children need to develop the parameters of a healthy relationship, but if they need gentle redirection and wise counsel to accomplish that, why wouldn't you want to do that for them? Doesn't that fall into the 'father' category? Is that an unrealistic expectation? I don't think so."

I am of the mind-set that regardless of the age of one's children, a father is always a father. I even asked my friend, "Don't you still need your father?"

He said, "Oh, I never thought of it like that. I see what you are saying."

The fruit doesn't fall far from the tree. One of the common fears that many face is the fear of public speaking. My fear of public speaking isn't as great as my fear of snakes, but that hasn't always been the case. I am terrified of snakes, and I used to be equally terrified of public speaking. Even though I speak publically on a weekly basis, I always get butterflies before I begin speaking. I am just hopeful they will fly in formation until I've said all I need to say.

Fear of public speaking is obviously a dominant gene I passed on to my daughter, but she is more proactive than I am. She will be the first to tell you she is terrified when she has to speak before a group.

My daughter has always been a "take charge kind of person." That trait is one of the characteristics she inherited from her mother. In order to nullify her fear of public speaking, she opted to join a Toastmasters group. She thought that would be a good faith effort to overcome the anxiety she experiences when she has to speak before a group.

It takes a lot of courage to purposefully put yourself in a situation that is very uncomfortable in order to develop the skill set to manage the discomfort in a more productive way. I was very proud of her for doing so.

Interestingly, the topic she chose for her first speech was entitled "Is It True, You Know, What They Say About Preacher's Kids?" I was intrigued with the title. She promised me that she was going to make it funny and promised to send me a copy of the speech after she presented it before the group.

A copy of the speech was not forthcoming, so I asked about it. "How did the speech go?"

She replied, "I think it was well-received. People laughed. I feel good about it."

"Great," I said. "So when do I get to read it?"

"Well, Dad, there's a problem..." followed by a period of silence.

"Did you say problem? Did you describe me in an unkind fashion?"

"Oh no, not at all," was her response. "I did share a funny story that you know nothing about. That is why I haven't sent you the speech because I'm afraid you'll be upset when you read it."

I assured her that if the event was over ten years ago, the statute of limitation on wrongdoings in her childhood had expired. "Send me the speech," I replied.

Despite knowing that there was nothing she could share that would offend me, I was a little anxious. Although I intuitively knew that she probably has driven the car 130 miles an hour, how could I fault her for that? I guess you have to chalk it up to "sins of the father." I also know that she once ran a traffic light because she knew the friend in front of her would go through the light. By the way, she was wrong about the friend in front of her. He stopped at the traffic light. She called me when a tow truck was needed to remove her car from the street.

When I finally received a copy of my daughter's speech, I was impressed. She made no pretense that "being a preacher's kid" was easy. As she stated, "There are certain expectations of what is, and more importantly, what is not acceptable behavior."

I was surprised by the openness and transparency she displayed in her communication. She stated, "My brother and I certainly weren't angels. With ten years in between our ages, we often had arguments and scuffles. On Sunday morning, however, we were the closest of allies.

"My brother and I often sat in the pew each week and listened in disbelief as our dad recounted our most embarrassing moments to the congregation. As payback for having to endure these uncomfortable moments, during the sermon, we would catch our dad's attention and then brush our hair aside. You could see worry building on my dad's face, and invariably he would run his fingers through his hair in an effort to attempt to fix what was actually in place. Victory was ours."

Her summation filled my heart with delight. "It is a true blessing to be a preacher's kid. My father is one of my best friends. I look to him for guidance and counsel. Every Sunday, I find myself in a pew in that same small, quaint church in Henly, Texas, knowing that at any moment, I could be the target of this week's sermon illustration."

Incidentally, the thing she worried about thinking I'd be upset over was a non-issue. I knew about it when it happened. I just opted to let it go. You have to pick your battles. Everything can't be an issue.

Apparently, there was an element of truth related to my daughter's observation that, at times, I used personal family situations as sermon illustrations. It was not long after that I was very surprised to learn that she coordinated plans with her brother for a special Father's Day celebration at church. My son and his family were visiting with us. I didn't know until I got to church for morning worship that my daughter had invited her brother to take my place in the pulpit and assume the responsibility for leading the worship service. I was totally unaware of their plans until I was instructed at church to take a seat with the congregation.

My son began, "I'd like to start by wishing a very happy Father's Day to all of the dads. A couple of weeks ago, my sister called to inform me that she'd like to give Dad a meritorious day off on Father's Day Sunday and inquired as whether or not I'd be willing to say a couple of words about Dad on Father's Day.

"I immediately felt a mischievous grin begin to form as I reflected back on all of the times that I sat out there with you as Dad utilized my most embarrassing moments as lead-ins to his sermons. It wasn't until after I had committed that I realized that we've been a part of this church community for thirty-plus years, and anything that Dad has done that would embarrass him, y'all already know and most likely were involved with as well.

"Faced with the dilemmas of not being able to utilize the 'bully pulpit' that I'd been granted to cause Dad a few uncomfortable moments, I decided that I'd better come up with something profound to share with you. Unfortunately for me, one of the Marine Corps' leadership principles is to know yourself and seek self-improvement…in other words, know your limitations…so I quickly scratched profound.

"However, since I was already in that part of the alphabet, and we're in the middle of another election year, I moved on to politics. I thought I'd share with you my thoughts on how our personal beliefs shape our political philosophies using Dad and me as examples. Now, Dad and I exemplify a phrase that was coined back in 2000…the 'Compassionate Conservative'…which is to say that Dad's compassionate and I'm conservative. When my idea of a meaningful discourse on political philosophy quickly fizzled, I decided that I'd just share a few of my thoughts about dads with you."

I was absolutely astonished at the insight and values that my son subsequently shared related to fatherhood. He took the time to acknowledge the debt of gratitude and thanksgiving he has for several of the men in our church family who were significant role models and persons of significance during his growing-up years. It carried with it the "it takes a village" approach to shape the life of a child.

Perhaps, the fruit doesn't fall far from the tree. The humor my son wove into his Father's Day presentation was not only attention getting, but it was very funny.

He went on to say, "I've heard that, as men, when we age and mature, we turn into our fathers, and I believe there is some truth to that. About ten years ago, my sister gave me one of the nicest compliments that I've ever received, although to be honest, I don't think she intended it that way at the time.

"Although I'd been a little rebellious as a teenager, I was at least predictable. My actions had in no way prepared my folks for what was to come when my sister hit her teens, because with her...all bets were off. At their wit's end, my folks asked me to speak with her about her behavior. While I was in the process of imparting on her the aforementioned expectations of acceptable behavior, she quickly cut me off and said, 'You sound just like Dad.'"

He concluded his comments by sharing what being a father has meant to him. "Honestly, I view it as the most important mission that I've ever undertaken. I believe that having a child is the most meaningful, wonderful, joyful experience a person can have. There isn't anything that I've found that compares with the first time you see your child or the first time they look at you and smile.

"At the same time, being a dad can be a daunting task. It is a tremendous responsibility and failure is not an option.

"At least at their present ages, in my kids' eyes, I can do no wrong. I can doctor scrapes and scratches, I can pull splinters, I can bait my own hook and most importantly, I can be counted on to give them snacks when, unbeknownst to me, their mother has already told them no.

"Being a dad is challenging, even frustrating at times. I am sure due in large part to the 'parental curse' that I believe all parents eventually pass along to their children. You know, the one that comes out in the heat of an argument where you say to your child, 'Someday, I hope you have a child that acts just like you.'"

My son concluded, "To you, fathers, I thank you once again. If I can do half the job of raising my own children, that you've done raising me, I'll consider my most important mission successfully completed."

Perhaps "the fruit doesn't fall far from the tree." Hopefully from a spiritual perspective, that is also the case. We are encouraged to ensure the fruit doesn't fall far from the tree. Paul wrote, "For those God foreknew he also predestined to be conformed to the likeness of his Son, that he might be the firstborn among many brothers" (Romans 8:29).

If we are pursuing life under the leadership and influence of the Spirit, our lives should be a mirror image of his life. Even Christ said of himself, "I tell you the truth, the Son can do nothing by himself; he can only do what he sees his Father doing, because whatever the Father does the Son also does. For the Father loves the Son and shows him all he does" (John 5:19–20). The approach we take to life should chronicle that of the Son. "Greater love has no one than this, that he lay down his life for his friends" (John 15:13). We are to be other-centered rather than preoccupied with our own little worlds.

Perhaps the litmus test for determining if our lives are lived according to his intent have some relationship to the "fruit not falling far from the tree." When we can reach the place that we can say with Christ, "I only do what I see the Father doing," it will be more than enough.

FAMILY OF FAITH

SEVERAL YEARS AGO, I had the privilege of walking though a dozen or so very old churches in Quebec City, Canada. I guess you could say I went to church. But in the dozen or so churches that I visited, there was only one church from which I emerged with the feeling that I had been to church.

When I walked into the St. Andrews Church, a Presbyterian church near the heart of the old city, I didn't expect it to differ from any of the other churches I had visited. Actually "visited" is probably not the most descriptive word; "toured" is probably a more accurate description of the experiences of the week I spent in Quebec City. Visit carries with it the connotation of some kind of connection; "toured" is more like walking through and not connecting with anything.

The St. Andrews Presbyterian Church was different. For one thing, it wasn't filled with people walking through and taking photographs of everything in sight. There were only three people in the church when I walked in, and they were volunteers to answer questions or provide the role of tour guide.

One of the volunteers, an older woman, took her role seriously. "Come on in. We don't bite."

I liked her invitation and bantered back, "You're in luck, I don't bite either."

After a few moments of looking around, the older lady asked, "Would you like to know something about the church or are you just here to look?"

That was pretty direct. How do you respond to a question like that? The only appropriate response had to be, "Yes, I'd like very much to know something about the church." That was like punching the crosswalk button on a light pole and turning the light green. This dedicated volunteer had a script to share, and she did it very well. It was pretty interesting.

One of the other volunteers, a much younger woman, hadn't said anything up to this point. I had the suspicion that she might be the pastor of the church and was observing the interaction. She seemed interested in the information that was being shared, but she was clearly yielding the presentation portion of the conversation to the older woman.

I was surprised when the younger woman asked where I attended church. I responded that I was only visiting the city, but that I attended a small Baptist church in Texas.

She responded that she and her family are Baptist, but that she attends St. Andrews because she likes the pastor and finds the sermons helpful. She said the Baptist church in Quebec City had been without a pastor for the past four years because they couldn't afford to pay a stipend, but that they still had Sunday school every Sunday and were supportive of one another.

She stated in matter-of-fact fashion that her husband had died several months earlier and that she had started worshipping at St. Andrews to hear the sermons. Her three children still preferred to go to the Baptist church to be with their friends and attend Sunday school. Consequently, the family was attempting to do both.

I expressed sympathy regarding the death of her husband and asked about her children. "Tell me about your children. How old are they? How are they managing the grief process? I know it has to be really tough for all of you." A simple empathetic response gave her the freedom to share their story.

We talked for well over an hour. Her husband was only forty-four when he died, and her three children were still very young (elementary and middle school ages). When I left there, it was my hope that I had contributed something in the conversation that was helpful and affirming about God's love and his ongoing ability to provide comfort and strength.

St. Andrews Church was the only church I toured (visited) and emerged feeling like I had been to church. I left there with a sense of God's care and support. It felt a lot like worship.

I've thought about the dozen or so churches I toured in Quebec City on more than one occasion. I've wondered what it would be like to be a part of that kind of church experience. I've also wondered if those churches are really places of worship or are they magnificent old buildings with a rich history and not a lot of relevancy for today?

Have you ever considered what it would be like to belong to a church that not only is a place of worship, but one that also doubles as an attraction for tourists who approach the venue as visiting a museum rather than an active place of worship?

Five or six years ago, our church started hosting the annual community homecoming in our fellowship hall. Prior to that time, the volunteer fire department was the site for such gatherings, and they were held in an open-air setting in the heat of the summer. Attendance wasn't always all the promoters hoped. I'm sure the lack of creature comforts in an outdoor setting had some impact on attendance.

As I recall, the year our church started hosting the community homecoming in our fellowship hall, it was packed with people. It was the largest homecoming gathering I remember, and I've been around for three and a half decades.

According to the journal notes I made following the celebration, it was a full day. It was a fun day. It was a day of renewing acquaintances, meeting new people, sharing stories, and to some degree, reliving the past for those who grew up in this locality. I was even surprised by some of the pictures on display. I had forgotten that I was ever young, thin, or had dark hair.

At different portions of the day, I watched as folks of yesteryear walked through our church (some I knew, most I didn't). It was almost as if for a brief moment our church took on the characteristics of a museum. All who toured were extremely complimentary...some couldn't believe how updated, comfortable, attractive, and well-kept the church was. Everyone loved the stained glass windows.

One lady said, "These pews are wonderful."

Then she asked, "Did you just put them in?" She seemed surprised when I said they had been here twenty-five to twenty-six years. She responded, "Well then, you must have just had them reupholstered. They look great!" (I didn't tell her, but I made a mental note to share that with the folks who think they need updating).

Some people I'd not met before expressed things like, "Oh, you are the pastor here. I've heard about you." After a pause that seemed a little long, they added, "you're doing a good job." I attempted to provide an honest response, "Actually, whoever you heard that from was just being kind.... The kindness of this family of faith is the only explanation I have for the ongoing privilege to be their pastor."

According to my journal, I awakened early the following morning thinking about the people who were in attendance. I also thought about the people who weren't present but would have been in attendance had health permitted.

In the early morning hours, I thought about the people who were present; people who live almost in the shadow of the church, but for whatever reason haven't attended in decades. Even more sadly, they aren't an active part of any church fellowship.

Do they see our church only as a museum reminding them of the wonderful, or perhaps not-so-wonderful, memories leftover from childhood? (So far, no one has verbalized anything related to "not-so-wonderful memories," but I think we have to leave that door open.)

That's not to say that what we represent no longer has relevancy for them. Some articulate that it does. But they live in a world where they are, by their own admission, simply too busy to devote a Sunday morning to worship with others.

In the early morning hours, I thought about the people who are here—here being our community, who were here for the homecoming—here being our church, but who are really not here or anywhere else for the purpose of worship, and it made me sad.

Did we fail them as a family of faith? Could we have done more? Should we, even now…years or decades later, pick up where we left off? Would you agree with me that it's the little things in life that make a difference?

More recently, I found myself engaged in a conversation with a man from the community who, based on my limited knowledge, is not engaged with a family of faith anywhere. He may not even be a person of faith. He asked me, "Don, how would coming to your church make me a better person?" I suspected the question was the introduction to what could prove to be a long-disputed dialogue, but I answered him honestly anyway. There was a surprised look on his face when I said, "It wouldn't. Coming to our church wouldn't make you a better person."

I went on to say that a relationship with God has nothing to do with our performance. It is all about our accepting the gift of life that is available to us through Christ. We don't come to church to get better. We come to church for focus (worship) and fellowship. People need people, and people need God. That is the reason we gather together. I invited him to join with us for the experience.

I am blessed to be a part of a family of faith who chooses to love one another and support their greatest good. I was recently asked at a wedding reception how long I have been pastor of our church. Every time I am asked that question and respond that it has been over thirty-plus years, it highlights for me how wonderfully blessed I am. Not many churches have a heritage that includes the longstanding patience to be content with the same pastor.

Ours has been a love relationship. My longevity is more about the family of faith than it is about me. Our folks are so incredibly kind, patient, supportive, encouraging, and loving. In essence, that summarizes some of the strengths of our church.

Occasionally, someone from another walk of my life will ask, "How's the church going?" I'm never really sure what they are asking.

- Are they asking about attendance? How full is the building?
- Do they want to know if attendance is more than last year or the year before that?
- Are they asking how we are doing compared to other churches?

Ours has been a long-term relationship. I first came to supply the pulpit on consecutive Sundays in late 1978. The church subsequently called me as pastor in February 1979. (Back in that day, I had dark brown hair that covered my ears and a full beard and big glasses. I probably looked very different from any pastor the church had ever had before. I can certainly understand their need to be cautionary before they called me as pastor).

I remember my son's first comments the Sunday I came in view of a call. It was the first Sunday he or his mother had accompanied me. We were active members of a large church in Austin. I really didn't know what my wife or son would think about a small church experience.

Before we were out of the parking lot, my son said, "Dad, you'd be crazy if you didn't want to come to church here. These people are really kind." And that was the beginning of a love relationship that has sustained our family across the years. My son was a second grader at the time. To give you a frame of reference, he is now a major in the US Marine Corps and will retire soon. Ours has been a long-term love affair.

My daughter and her husband share that same level of enthusiasm and commitment to our church and to the community. They recently bought acreage in the area with the intent to make this locality their home. They love it here.

I have friends who don't think we are a Baptist church because Baptist churches don't keep the same pastor for a lifetime. Even some of the people I know who live in the community who don't come to church and who don't like preachers, generally think I'm okay.

In addition to responsibilities at church, I also have a full-time job that I dearly love. The demands are sometimes grueling, and between the two, I don't have a lot of time for many other interests. However, I love what I'm doing, so I really never work a day in my life.

In the truest sense, my church relationship is primarily the long-term therapy program God has enrolled me in to promote growth and healing and help me become the man God intends. I am extremely blessed.

One of my greatest fears is that I will stay beyond my usefulness. I can't think of anything I would rather not happen than that. Despite my intent to be cautionary in that regard, I think we are good for now. I truthfully can't think of a place I'd rather be.

The family of faith is important. It is the baseline for establishing love relationships that endure the test of time, a venue for building on our strengths and relinquishing dependency on those areas of our life where we need the transformation that only God can provide and the venue for sharing his hope with others. It really is more than enough.

LOOKING BACK

ONE OF MY favorite all-time movies is *Remains of the Day*. Before you download the movie for viewing, I must tell you it didn't even make the "honorable mention" category with my wife. She thought it was extremely boring. I have watched the movie several times. I always find it the catalyst for reflection and thought.

The movie is the story of a "workaholic" older English butler who invested his life managing the household of his employer. In the realm of his employment, he gave top priority to work-related tasks. In the process, he failed to successfully manage the relationship building dimensions of his personal life. The movie is basically an overview of the butler looking back over his life and reflecting on misplaced priorities. I found it extremely thought-provoking and interesting.

From time to time I, too, purposefully take time out to simply reflect on life. Often, the catalyst for reflection is a quest for learning. My prayer is often, "God, what am I supposed to learn from this." It may surprise you, but sometimes the question is prompted by the realization of how wonderfully fulfilling my life is rather than a response to difficulty or disappointment.

Truthfully, everything I've experienced in life has worked together for good. The highs and lows of my experiences have all contributed to my sense of well-being and purpose. No doubt that is true for each of us.

Back when my oldest granddaughter was four years old, she consistently found herself wanting only one thing. She wanted a baby sister. She told her mother, "If you'll just have a baby sister for me, I'll take care of her." Despite the fact that she was only four, she had all the confidence that she'd be able to keep her commitment. She really wanted a baby sister.

Consequently, when her parents subsequently shared the news months later that they were having another baby, Jenna was as thrilled as the grandparents. There was nothing she wanted more than a baby sister (unless it was to have her ears pierced, which also ranked pretty high on her wish list—that led me to realize that I'm too old for parenting. Getting her ears pierced wouldn't be a consideration if I got to cast the deciding vote).

A couple of weeks before her first sonogram, my daughter-in-law, who is an exceptionally sensitive and child-oriented parent, talked to both Jenna and William about the importance of the doctor's visit and that they would then know if the baby is going to be a sister or brother. Jenna had never considered the possibility of a brother...this was not good news! She announced with marked determination, "If it's a brother, I'm not going to love him and I'm not going to hold him. I only want a sister."

Consequently, when the day of the doctor's appointment arrived, it proved to be a day of bitter disappointment for Jenna. She learned that the long hoped for baby sister was going to be a baby brother instead. It is an understatement to say that the news was not well received.

In the mind and heart of a four-year-old, how could such a terrible mistake be made? She didn't want a brother. She wanted a sister. From her perspective, it wasn't fair and it certainly wasn't what she wanted to hear. The news was accompanied with a flood of tears and some very real emotion.

Later in the day, when Jenna had a litany of questions about how such an awful mistake could be made, her mother responded, "We really don't get to decide. God decides if we need a boy or a girl." With the kind of honesty most of us are incapable of revealing, Jenna responded, "If God gets to decide, God cheated us."

Four years later, Jenna would have absolutely no recall of ever wanting a baby sister instead of a younger brother. She relishes her role as big sister to both William and Jake. She moved immediately from wanting a little sister to wanting a collection of American Girl dolls. Consequently, I shudder every Christmas knowing her Christmas wish list will rank high on her Gram's shopping spree.

Despite the times that I, too, have momentarily had the passing thought that "God cheated us," I've also subsequently made the discovery that through it all, he has been in the midst of whatever life brought my way.

In my teenage years, I felt God's call on my life to be a pastor. Consequently, I initially went to school with the intent of one day becoming a pastor. My subsequent tenure in graduate school was interrupted with a draft notice from the US Army. My wife and I moved back to our hometown so she could be near family while I was away.

Things didn't turn out as planned. I subsequently failed my military physical and was denied the opportunity to serve my country. Reportedly, instead of going *pitter-patter*, my heart goes "patter-pit." A diagnosis of a "right bundle branch block" eliminated me from consideration by the military.

At that juncture in my life, I shifted my focus and thought it would be refreshing to simply have a job. I looked to see what kind of work was available and eventually landed a job as a child protective services caseworker.

In many respects, the human services field is different today than when I began working for the Texas Department of Public Welfare more than forty years ago. During the ensuing forty-plus years, there have been dramatic changes in child welfare systems, in our values concerning families, and in our understanding of what is critically important for healthy child development.

Of course, some things in the human services field remained unchanged. I have no difficulty recalling that office space was inadequate, the workload was almost impossible to manage, and everything was crisis-oriented. A child protective service caseload included a myriad of different services to a child or family in need. Yet in reflecting back, I cannot help remembering those early years with a degree of fondness.

My early days as a child welfare worker were filled with variety. The workload included abuse/neglect investigations and sorting out what needed to be done to offer a veil of protection to children, maintaining an ongoing caseload of support services to families in crisis, supervision of children in foster care, and the occasional placement of a newborn in adoption. The work was fascinating. It was also important.

Those early experiences redefined ministry for me. For the first time in my life, I had the ongoing sense that my work made a difference for children and families needing help. I was young and idealistic and went home in the evening with the sense my work was purposeful. It carried with it an ongoing sense that I had found my niche. The desire to pastor became secondary to my new sense of calling. I still wanted to serve God, but I had discovered a new venue in which to fulfill that task.

On occasion, I still think about the children and experiences from that early child protective services caseload. I sometimes wonder what became of them. I remember their names, their circumstances, and the service plans we collectively put in place.

Back before I had children of my own, I participated in a number of infant adoptions. I named one little guy Jean Paul by combining the first names of two of my co-workers. He is memorable for a couple of reasons. The adoptive family selected for his placement lived out of state. Consequently, I was totally responsible for Jean Paul's care during the period of time it took to travel from Texas to a very distant city. I had never carried a diaper bag before or had to concern myself with things like formula, etc. You would have thought I was a doting parent if you had seen the two of us together. Secondly, it was the first time I had traveled by airplane.

On more than one occasion, I've wondered about the childhood Jean Paul subsequently experienced and about what type of adult he became. It is always a source of delight for me when I receive information regarding any of the children I've previously served.

Not long ago, I received a photo of a two-year-old girl and her newborn brother. The little girl was wearing glasses and looked exactly like her mother did when she came into foster care at the age of two. That was twenty-plus years ago. Her foster parents subsequently adopted her. Today, this young mother with two precious children is proof that the generational cycle of abuse and family crisis can be changed. The privilege of being a part of that process is both very humbling and gratifying.

At times, I have to confess that I am like the "workaholic" older English butler who invested too much of his life in his work. If I could hit the rewind button and play it forward again, I'd work toward finding more balance between my work life, my family life, my church life, opportunities for growth and development, recreation and new discoveries. I haven't always gotten it right.

Sometimes when I'm stopped at a traffic light and notice someone carrying a sign stating, "Homeless Will Work For Food," I have the passing thought, "What makes me different from them?" In reality, there is probably nothing. I have been blessed a thousand times over, and it simply is a result of God's grace. I haven't done anything to deserve it. It is a gift freely given. I need to be careful not to take any of it for granted.

All of my life, I have been surrounded by capable, loving, supportive individuals who have added much to the quality of my life. I am simply an ordinary, everyday kind of guy who is the recipient of much love. I am still waiting to discover something of significance to add to the world, but in the interim, I am content to simply live life one day at a time. Maybe it is true that the most significant thing you can do is simply show up.

I have been given the gift of an incredible family. It is interesting that both my son and daughter have voluntarily signed on to ensure some level of responsibility to make sure we are okay. I personally don't think my wife or I need someone looking over our shoulder to ensure our personal safety or well-being. We are both independent and very capable of embracing life to the fullest. It is interesting that both children seemingly know our schedule and if we vary from it greatly they sound an alarm bell. The other evening, I received a text message from my daughter: "Where are you and mom? Craig called, and he is concerned that you are not at home." We were out for a late dinner, and I didn't notice that my son had called my cell phone. When we didn't answer at home or on my cell phone, he called his sister to ask our whereabouts. My son lives in North Carolina. He doesn't need to worry about whether we make it home before curfew.

I know so many adults my age who are alienated from their adult children. It saddens me that family relationships have to be as difficult as a lot of people choose to make them. I can't take any credit for being the recipient of my children's love, but I don't take it for granted. I am loved well beyond my deserving. What is true of my children is also true of my daughter-in-law and son-in-law. We are the recipients of their love. What a feel-good experience!

My wife and I choose to make our home available as the gathering place for any extended family at any time. Consequently, ours is the setting for many family gatherings. It is nice when grandchildren want to come to Texas to Granddad's house. It always makes me feel good to hear that. It makes me even feel better when they are here.

Even my twin brother's daughter, Karoni, and her family think of our home as their home. Lilian, her daughter, is as much one of our grandchildren as my son's children. We love them equally. We love them the same.

A couple of years ago, I received a telephone call from my niece asking for help. Karoni had confirmed her acceptance of the invitation extended her by the National League of Families to present the invocation at the annual meeting in Washington, DC. The National League of Families was established as an organization to advocate for a full accounting of POW/MIAs from the Vietnam conflict. Karoni was only two years old when her dad's plane went down in Vietnam during the "Christmas bombing raids of 1972."

When Karoni mentioned to a friend that she had no idea what she would share in terms of a prayer, the friend suggested she "outsource the project to one of her dad's brothers since both are preachers."

Instead of looking for quality, she opted to go with convenience since she sees me often and her other uncle lives out of state. My initial response was mostly tongue-in-cheek and was something closely akin to:

Dear Heavenly Father,

In many ways we now know how the children of Israel must have felt after wandering around in the wilderness for forty years. Many of the families represented here have invested years of trust, emotions, energy and hopes only to emerge with a sense that we are no closer in our pilgrimage than when we started decades ago. We come each year believing that we are on the brink of bringing closure to the mystery surrounding our loved ones. Year after year many of us are told by governmental authorities and military personnel that crash sites have been determined, excavation plans have been made, funding for excavation has been secured and that sometime in the next few months, actual recovery will begin. Those promises repeatedly fail to materialize.

Just as the children of Israel needed "manna from heaven" to sustain their needs, we ask that you'd continue to provide us strength and the courage to go on. More importantly, we ask that you'd intervene and miraculously assist in tearing down the walls of opposition and orchestrate the recovery of our loved ones. For us, the "Promised Land" is synonymous to a "homecoming and final resting place for our loved ones."

For it's in your name that we pray. Amen.

Karoni laughed approvingly at my impromptu attempt to come up with an appropriate prayer, but I recognized that she would probably decide that "discretion is the better part of valor" and contact her other uncle for a rendering that might be more politically correct.

Surprisingly, I later learned that she presented the prayer exactly as I had written it. Apparently no one was offended. She was asked again to deliver the prayer this past year. She again outsourced the writing of the prayer, but this time, I simply put in writing what I already knew was in her heart.

Dear Heavenly Father,

We ask that you would give us an awareness of your presence as we meet today. We are grateful for your promise never to leave or forsake us.

In looking back across our journey, we cannot deny that you have been faithful to your Word. As we come to pray, I want to express gratitude to you for the League of Families.

For many, the League of Families has become an extended family where friendship and support are second nature. Not only have we known the pain of separation from loved ones separated from us by war, but in the midst of our grief, we have also discovered the compassion and friendship of other League family members who share the same pilgrimage.

The Scriptures tell us when one member suffers, then all suffer together. Certainly as League members, we have each been strengthened by the collective support we share.

Truthfully, I was a toddler when I was thrust into the quagmire of grief and uncertainty related to the fate of my father. Across the years, I've come to the gradual acceptance of his fate and trust your goodness for his future. One day we will be eternally reunited. For that I am most thankful.

We thank you Father for the League of Family members who have been able to bring closure to the very long and painful chapter of their lives through the return of the remains of their loved ones.

For others of us who still wait, we are grateful for your presence and support. We also acknowledge that our lives have been enriched through the friendships and sense of family we share as a League of Family.

Please direct and guide as we share this time together.

For it's in Christ's name we pray. Amen.

One of the wonderful strengths shared by our family is our commitment to maintain a sense of family and provide support and encouragement to one another. I never take for granted that I am the recipient of much love. The love and honor I receive from family members is a gift that I cherish and will never take for granted. I see too many of my friends who don't have that same wonderful sense of heritage.

If there has been a surprise in my life, it is the recent awareness that my children grew up with a sense of obligation or expectation related to being a preacher's kid. That surprises me because I have never ever thought of myself as a preacher. Actually, if you could hear me on Sunday morning, you probably wouldn't either.

I simply have had the wonderful privilege of serving in a church where I am loved. It has been one of the delights of my life. I know painfully well that the church will not have a perfect pastor as long as I am allowed the privilege. I don't always get it right.

That is not to say that I am content with the status quo. I don't have to do an in-depth self-assessment to realize that I am sometimes opinionated and not necessarily as the result of divine appointment. No doubt there are times that I, too, am guilty of situation ethics to enhance myself rather than supporting the greater good of the community. I don't have to throw too many stones at the "religious right" before I become obsessed and contaminated with that which I detest.

At some level, I am hopeful that my life will continue down the course that has already been charted. I desire for nothing more than what I've already received. My life is full, and I long for nothing more. Yet at the same time, I am open to God's ultimate desire in the outcome of my life. Although I don't have the ability to envision life more fulfilling or rewarding than what I've already experienced, ultimately God is in control. Left to my own discretion, I routinely make a mess of things. It works best if I yield to his leadership. I know from a lifetime of experience that I can trust in the proven dependability of God's love. I am content to play it forward and trust that God will be glorified in the process. I am holding on to the promise that his power is made perfect in weakness. It really is more than enough.

BIBLIOGRAPHY

Anderson, Marian. "My Lord What a Morning." Kirkus Review. October 25, 1956. https://www.kirkusreviews.com/book-reviews/marian-anderson/my-lord-what-a-morning/.

Anderson, Marian. "My Lord What a Morning." Marian Anderson. Eleanor Roosevelt. WGBH American Experience. PBS. http://www.pbs.org/wgbh/americanexperience/features/biography/eleanor-anderson/.

Bencke, Wanda. "Christmas in Heaven." Comfort-For-Bereavement.com. http://www.comfort-for-bereavement.com/Christmas.html.

Brokaw, Tom. *The Greatest Generation.* New York: Random House, 1998. http://www.amazon.com/The-Greatest-Generation-Tom-Brokaw/dp/0812975294

Brokaw, Tom. *The Greatest Generation.* New York: Random House, 1998. Front Flap.

Brown, H. Jackson. *Life's Little Instruction Book.* Nashville, Tenn.: Rutledge Hill Press, 1991.

Chester, Scott. "Lovely Rose at 87." Lovely Rose at 87. May 31, 2005. www.schester.com/2005/05/31/lovely-rose-at87/.

Christopherson, John, and Matt Apuzzo. "Conn. Town Mourns as Police Look for Answers." *The Daytona Beach News Journal*. December 15, 22012. http://www.news-journalonline.com/article/20121215/WIRE/312159969/0/search?p=2&tc=pg.

"Conscience Fund." Wikipedia. October 9, 2014.

Denison, James. "Finding Your Soul." First Baptist Church, Midland, Texas (sermon). May 24, 1992.

Diamond, Neil. "I Am…I Said." Neil Diamond Lyrics. http://www.azlyrics.com/lyrics/neildiamond/iamisaid.html.

"Don't Laugh at Me." Summer of Monuments. http://en.wikipedia.org/wiki/Don't_Laugh_at_Me.

"Édith Piaf." Wikipedia. January 10, 2014.

"Forgiveness." Forgiveness. http://www.valueoptions.com/august04_newsletter/forgiveness.htm.

Gilgoff, Dan, and Eric Marrapodi. "Massacre of Children Leaves Many Asking 'Where's God?'" CNN Religion. blogs.cnn.com. December 14, 2912. http://religion.blogs.cnn.com/2012/12/14/massacre-of-children-leaves-many-asking-wheres-god/.

Greenwood, Lee. "God Bless the USA." Lee Greenwood. http://www.azlyrics.com/lyrics/leegreenwood/godblesstheusa.html.

"Interesting—the Most Interesting Man in the World." The New Yorker. http://www.newyorker.com/magazine/2011/02/07/interesting.

Jack C. Longley, Pastor of Trinity Presbyterian Church, San Jose, CA from September 1978 – April 2009. "Things I've Learned" included in message #1091, "Don't Walk…Run on the Road God Has Called You to Travel." April 3, 2005.

Jones, Alicea. "Child at Heart Stays Busy in Round Rock." *The Williamson County Sun*, March 7, 2010, Faith sec.

Livingston, Gordon. *Too Soon Old, Too Late Smart: Thirty True Things You Need to Know Now.* New York: Marlowe & Co., 2004.

Lucado, Max. "Max Lucado Pens Prayer in Response to Connecticut School Tragedy." Examiner.com. http://www.examiner.com/article/max-lucado-pens-prayer-response-to-connecticut-school-tragedy.

Lucado, Max. "Wet Feet." In *Grace More Than We Deserve Greater Than We Imagine*, 59. Nashville: Thomas Nelson, 2012.

Lucado, Max. *He Chose the Nails: What God Did to Win Your Heart.* Nashville: Word Pub., 2000. 106.

McGinnis, Alan Loy. *The Friendship Factor.* Minneapolis: Augsburg Fortress, 2004. 30.

Miranda Warning. January 1, 1966. http://en.wikipedia.org/wiki/Miranda_warning.

Ogilvie, Lloyd John. *If God Cares, Why Do I Still Have Problems?* Waco, Tex.: Word Books, 1985. 180–181.

Ortberg, John. "God's Great Desire." In *God Is Closer Than You Think*, 14. Grand Rapids: Zondervan, 2005.

Ortberg, John. *God Is Closer Than You Think.* Grand Rapids: Zondervan, 2005. Inside cover.

Ortberg, John. *If You Want to Walk on Water, You've Got to Get out of the Boat.* Grand Rapids, Mich.: Zondervan Pub. House, 2001. 35.

Ortberg, John. *The Life You've Always Wanted: Spiritual Disciplines for Ordinary People.* Grand Rapids, Mich.: Zondervan Pub. House, 1997. 82–83.

Ortberg, John. *When the Game Is Over, It All Goes Back in the Box.* Grand Rapids, Mich.: Zondervan, 2007. 84.

Reid, Harold W., and Don S. Reid. The Statler Brothers. "Class of '57." January 1, 1972. http://www.metrolyrics.com/class-of-57-lyrics-the-statler-brothers.html.

Rogers, Matt. "When Answers Aren't Enough." Mattrogers. us. http://www.mattrogers.us/books/when-answers-arent-enough/.

"Should We Fire God?" Jimpace.us. http://www.jimpace.org/should-we-fire-god/.

Siegel, Bernie S. *Prescriptions for Living: Inspirational Lessons for a Joyful, Loving Life*. New York: HarperCollins Publishers, 1998.

"Six-Word Memoirs Can Say It All." CBSNews. February 26, 2008. http://www.cbsnews.com/news/six-word-memoirs-can-say-it-all/.

Stanley, Andy. *The Principle of the Path: How to Get from Where You Are to Where You Want to Be*. Nashville, Tenn.: Thomas Nelson, 2008. 19.

Stock, Gregory. *The Book of Questions*. New York: Workman Pub., 1987.

Swindoll, Charles R. "Part II Mid-Winter's Blast." In *Come before Winter—and Share My Hope*. Portland, Or.: Multnomah Press, 1985.

Waits, Tom. "Tom Waits–Georgia Lee." Song Meanings. http://songmeanings.com/songs/view/3530822107858535999/.

Yancey, Philip, and Paul W. Brand. *The Gift of Pain: Why We Hurt & What We Can Do about It, 12*. Grand Rapids, Mich: Zondervan Publ., 1997.

PHOTOS

Bill & Lena Forrester - Paternal Grandparents

Craig - in Christmas Pkgn

Craig and Becky Forrester

Craig Homecoming - Christmas 2012

Don, Treva & Craig

Donnie & Ronnie

Andrea and Kevin

Forrester Family

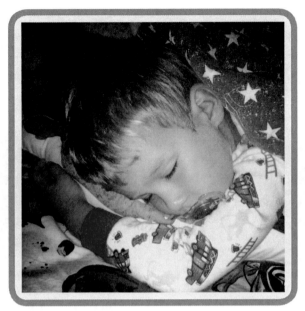

Jake with Daddy Doll

Kids on Swing

Larry Forrester

Lilian Gonzales & Jenna Forrester

Lilian Gonzales

Lt. Col. Adam Chalkley & Craig - Afghanistan

Luther and Margie Demoss - Maternal Grandparents

Ronnie & Donnie

Ronnie, Larry & Donnie

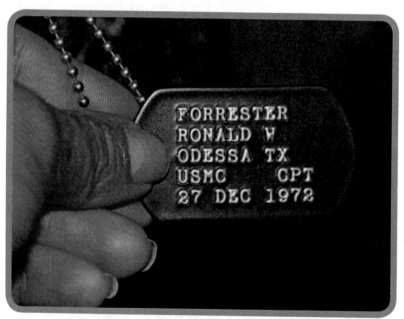

Ronnie's Dog Tag from Display at Capitol